Praise for

Single Today

"*Single Today* is a brave and stirring look into the deep waters of the human heart. It asks probing questions and explores underlying pressures of marital expectations from the church and society. We are led by the thoughtful and vulnerable reflections of Wekenman's own journey, as he lays his heart to bear. And what he models for us is vulnerability, integrity, and deep understanding. Yes, this is a book about being single, but it is even more about being truly present and soaking up every bit of beauty that the past and the future might otherwise steal. Ryan says he is good at being single, but the truth is, Ryan is good at living well, and this book invites us all to do the same."
—JEFFREY TACKLIND, author of *The Winding Path of Transformation,* and pastor of Little Church by the Sea, Laguna Beach

"Wekenman's vulnerability and openness exemplify that this was a book and a message that he *had* to write—not because he wanted to but out of a deep desire for himself and others to feel less alone in their unique callings in life. *Single Today* will be an encouragement to many who need to know that they are unique, gifted, valued, and loved."
—BEN HIGGINS, co-founder and president of Generous International and author of *Alone in Plain Sight*

"I've been a mentor for single women for more than a decade, and I wish I had this practical resource to share with them sooner! It's funny, warm, and encouraging, and it reads like you're having coffee with a good friend who also happens to be one of the wisest people you know. *Single Today* will change the way you see your past and your future, your singleness and yourself."
—STEPHANIE MAY WILSON, author of *Create a Life You Love*

"*Single Today* offers a vision for a fully satisfied life sans the need to be tethered relationally in marriage. It is the book every single person needs to read and every married person needs to read to better equip their single friends and family members to live the full lives God calls them to."
—WAYNE FRANCIS, lead pastor of The Life Church, New York; co-author of *God and Race;* and chaplain for the Brooklyn Nets

"Such a helpful guide for anyone struggling with contentment right now. I loved Wekenman's insight and stories that anyone can relate to, whether single, dating, engaged, or married."
—RUTH SOUKUP, *New York Times* bestselling author of *Living Well, Spending Less* and *Do It Scared*

"Wekenman clearly and brilliantly helps his readers learn to appreciate their single stage of life—not to reluctantly embrace it but to thrive in it and even be thankful for it! Singleness doesn't need to be a valley in life you must endure until you find that other person, but instead it can be a nonstop collection of mountaintop moments, inspired by God for your life, that you can be absolutely grateful for!"
—SHAWN JOHNSON, senior pastor of Red Rocks Church and author of *Attacking Anxiety*

"Wekenman shares from a deep place of knowing and understanding the experience and challenges faced by singles, whether they are feeling stuck, struggling with being single again, or loving it. Brilliantly written, this timely, inspiring, and biblically based work is full of practical application that will move readers to a place of true contentment in the season they are in."
—JIMMY AND IRENE ROLLINS, founders of TWO=ONE marriage ministry

"This book is packed with immediately practical real talk about contentment, purpose, and living presently through singleness, regardless of the reason or the season. *Single Today* is raw, relatable, and encouraging. It's the real deal."

—GRANGER SMITH, speaker and *New York Times* bestselling author of *Like a River*

"Wekenman's authenticity in *Single Today* will be a refreshing reminder of God's purpose for you in this season. The stereotypical eye-roll moments of singlehood are replaced with engaging stories of wrestling, hope, and wondering what more God has. Wekenman gives practical steps toward significant mindset shifts that lead to a deep satisfaction in being single today."

—JONATHAN POKLUDA, lead pastor, bestselling author, and host of *Becoming Something* podcast

Single Today

Single Today

Conquer Yesterday's Regrets,
Ditch Tomorrow's Worries, and
Thrive Right Where You Are

RYAN WEKENMAN

WaterBrook

Names in some anecdotes and stories have been changed to protect the identities of the persons involved.

A WaterBrook Trade Paperback Original

Published in the United States by WaterBrook, an imprint of Random House, a division of Penguin Random House LLC.

WATERBROOK and colophon are registered trademarks of Penguin Random House LLC.

LIBRARY OF CONGRESS CATALOGING-IN-PUBLICATION DATA

Names: Wekenman, Ryan, author.
Title: Single today: conquer yesterday's regrets, ditch tomorrow's worries, and thrive right where you are / Ryan Wekenman.
Description: [Colorado Springs] : WaterBrook, [2024] | Includes bibliographical references.
Identifiers: LCCN 2023028647 | ISBN 9780593600948 (trade paperback) | ISBN 9780593600955 (ebook)
Subjects: LCSH: Single people—Religious life. | Single people—Conduct of life.
Classification: LCC BV4596.S5 W45 2024 | DDC 248.8/4—dc23/eng/20231108
LC record available at https://lccn.loc.gov/2023028647

Printed in the United States of America on acid-free paper

waterbrookmultnomah.com

9 8 7 6 5 4 3 2 1

Most WaterBrook books are available at special quantity discounts for bulk purchase for premiums, fundraising, and corporate and educational needs by organizations, churches, and businesses. Special books or book excerpts also can be created to fit specific needs. For details, contact specialmarketscms@ penguinrandomhouse.com.

To my future spouse (jk, lol)

Do not worry about tomorrow.

—Jesus

Contents

Introduction: Two Enemies of Singleness   *3*

Part 1 | Yesterday   *9*

1   Stagnant Water
    Feel Your Feelings and Talk It Out   *15*

2   The Ones That Got Away
    Give It a Name, Give It Some Space, Let It Go   *32*

3   Sex, Shame, and Stoners
    Find Out What You're Medicating   *52*

4   The Happiest Place on Earth
    Set Up a System That Stirs   *72*

Mary's Interlude (Act 1): Stir the Stagnant Water   *89*

Part 2 | Tomorrow   *95*

5   The Tomorrow Trap
    Develop a Plan for the Panic   *99*

6   Bring the Wine
    Outsmart the Shot Clock   *116*

7   Less Grasping, More Laughing
    How to Let Go When You Start Overthinking   *133*

8   Rediscover Wonder
    Where to Find Wonder When You're Single   *148*

Mary's Interlude (Act 2): Still the Rough Water   *162*

Part 3 | Today *167*

9   The Kingdom of Me

Stop Putting Yourself at the Center of the Story *171*

10   Conflict, Connection, and Contentment

Discover the Benefits of True Community *185*

11   Single, Not Alone

Experience the Gift of Good Friends *201*

12   Flip the Script on Singleness

Stop Waiting for Permission *212*

Mary's Interlude (Act 3): Share What You Have *232*

Epilogue: Single-Minded *237*

Acknowledgments *241*

Notes *245*

Single Today

Introduction

Two Enemies of Singleness

Everyone is single at some point.

The young woman who has never been asked on a date.
The middle-aged man who gets blindsided by divorce.
The widow waking up in her bed by herself for the first time in decades.

Some hate it; others love it.
Some expect it; others get caught off guard by it.
Some are single intentionally; others are single reluctantly.
Some are single for a season; others are single for a reason.

Singleness is an old friend to some and an unexpected guest to others.

I suppose I'm somewhere in between the two. I've been single all thirty-four years of my life—longer than some, not nearly as long as others. I love being single. I love it so much that I want to be single the rest of my life.

That last sentence is completely true 82 percent of the time.[1] That's how I feel most hours of the day. But then there are other times. The nights I push my introversion to the limit and start feeling lonely, questioning if singleness is really what I want. Or the times I hang out with my niece and nephew and drive home wondering if I really want to miss out on having a family of my own. Or the moments I meet a couple who has been married for so long that they have that different kind of love—the kind that can be built only out of years of trust—and realize I'd miss out on experiencing that.

Saying yes to singleness means saying no to a lot of beautiful things about life. You can't say yes to the 82 percent without saying no to the 18 percent.

And then we need to consider the deeper layers of this topic. Like how some people have desired to be married since they were young but, decades later, still aren't.

Maybe that's you, and you picked up this book because you're frustrated (or should I say downright irritated?) with singleness. You want to get married, and you've put in the work. You know what you want and have made your list, checked it twice, prayed, even tried fasting that one time, and still nothing. You keep working on yourself, only to find out that no one else seems to be doing the same, so now the whole topic just makes your blood boil.

Maybe you're reading this book because you feel stuck. When you're in a relationship, you want to be single, and when you're single, you want to be in a relationship. You don't know how to move forward, yet you feel the deep despair of loneliness when you're by yourself and start asking all those existential questions about life and love and whether or not there's any purpose to any of this if you don't have a partner.

Maybe you picked up this book because you're single again for the first time in a long time, and the last time you were single, the world looked very different. Now you're trying to find your footing after heartbreak, heartache, or tragedy, and you don't even know where to begin.

No matter what your story is, we all have something in common. Every single person in the world understands that singleness is a struggle. We try to dress it up like it's not, but it is.

But you're not alone. There are billions of us. Billions of single people with billions of questions about billions of challenges.

So I present the questions this book gravitates around: *Is there a solution to all the struggles of singleness? Is there a way to live a full, abundant life on your own? Can you really love life without a love life?*

The simple answer is yes.
But simple doesn't mean easy.
We can't just ignore all the struggles and hope they go away. Instead, we must come face-to-face with them.

This book is my attempt to organize those billions of struggles into two categories.

Over the years, I've noticed a pattern. After hundreds of pastoral meetings with other single people, I eventually realized that just about every battle, fear, and insecurity single people deal with is caused by one of two things—what I call the two enemies of singleness:

> Enemy 1: yesterday (shame, regret, or sorrow about the past)
> Enemy 2: tomorrow (fear about the future)

Yesterday keeps us stuck replaying mistakes instead of moving forward. Second-guessing decisions from the past instead of focusing on the ones in front of us. Ruminating on betrayal or rejection, copying those experiences and pasting them onto new people we meet, and remaining closed off to new opportunities. *Will this pain ever go away? Am I broken beyond repair? Am I doomed to repeat the same mistakes?*

And then tomorrow makes us worry. (That's true for everyone, but when you're single, the future has some extra ammo to harass you with.) *Am I running out of time? Will all the good ones be taken? If all my friends get married but I stay single, will our friendships change? What about kids? Am I missing my opportunity to have a family?* Throw in a healthy dose of parental and societal pressure to fit a certain mold in a certain timeline, and it feels impossible to take a breath and be present today.

Yesterday pins us to the floor while tomorrow beats us up—the two make a deadly combo. As you're about to find out, that's my story. I've had plenty of bouts with the two enemies of singleness, and they used to win every fight. But they don't anymore. They still attack, but I have the tools I need to fight back. This book is going to equip you to do the same.

In part 1, we'll learn how to confront the first enemy—yesterday. The pain from the past that keeps us stuck isn't permanent. We aren't doomed to spend the rest of our lives ruminating. We can heal, forgive, and leave yesterday in the past.

In part 2, we'll take on the second enemy—tomorrow. *Surrender* is one of those words we throw around a lot in church, but it's easier to preach than practice, especially when you're single. We're going to practice it together.

Finally, part 3 is about today. The goal is not just to face the two enemies of singleness but also to experience the abundant life on the other side—to tap into the potential that today is teeming with.

At the end of each part, there's an interlude about Mary of Bethany. Mary is a beautiful character in the Bible who had three fascinating interactions with Jesus, each illustrating one of the parts of this book well. I could be wrong, but since there's no mention in Scripture of Mary having a husband or kids, I think that's a strong indication that she was single at the time. Whatever the reason for her singleness, I assume she was asking a lot of the same questions we are. As her story unfolds, my hope is you'll begin to see your story in hers.

Whether you end up being single for two more days, two more decades, or the rest of your life, this book is for you. Your single-ness is an incredible gift; you just have to put in some work to enjoy it. Along the way, you may meet someone who has been putting in the same work, and it may lead to an amazing relation-ship. Or you may not. That's the beauty of this book: It's about finding the type of contentment that doesn't require anyone else.

As we go along, I'm going to share my story as a single pastor try-ing (and sometimes failing) to live it well. I'm not good at much, but I am good at being single. The best way I can help you on your path is to share the beautifully difficult journey I went on (and am still going on) to thrive as a single person today.

Ultimately, this is a book about today. It's about surrendering your future and learning to see this present moment as the gift that it is. The full, abundant life you're searching for is available while you're single. It's time to conquer yesterday's regrets, ditch tomorrow's worries, and be single today.

PART ONE

Yesterday

Forget the former things;
do not dwell on the past.
—Isaiah 43:18

"THE POOL WILL BE CLOSED until further notice."

That was the extent of the email my homeowners' association sent me last year—they've never been much for small talk. And although I respect a one-sentence note, I'd love for it to be followed with "Don't worry. We'll also decrease your monthly payment." That never happens. Amenities come and go, but fees are forever.

I spend a lot of time at my pool—enough to know the maintenance is done every Friday by a couple who pull up in a white F-150, the bed overflowing with chemicals, gadgets, and all sorts of equipment that helps them keep the water looking and smelling fresh.

I don't know their names, but let's call them Jeff and Judy. They add chemicals, check levels, clean filters, and stir the water. Or at least they used to. After we received that notorious email, Jeff and Judy stopped showing up.

For the first week after the notice went out, everything seemed fine. I'd run past the pool and consider jumping the fence and swimming anyway. But around week three, the water had a green tint. After another week, there was algae on the surface. And by the end of the second month, the pool was completely green. It looked and smelled awful, like a swamp.

My HOA taught me a valuable lesson—stagnant water starts to stink. Because when Jeff and Judy stopped showing up to stir the water, the pool began its gradual descent from refreshing to repulsive.

That picture of my pool turning into a swamp is the central metaphor for part 1. Imagine your soul as a body of water, like my pool during good times: clear, clean, refreshing water. That's the state our souls are created for. The problem is, life happens. People pollute it, we ignore it, and it starts to stink.

Ignoring the pain, shame, and insecurities from your past is like my neighborhood ignoring the pool. It seems fine initially, but eventually, the living water becomes a stagnant swamp.

Your soul requires upkeep, and one of the beautiful things about a relationship is you have another person built into your life, keeping the water stirred—a Jeff or Judy, if you will. You have a significant other who is constantly asking you about your day, giving you space to process the good, the bad, and the ugly. And you have a responsibility to do the same for them. They help you get your eyes off yourself and devote your life to someone else, and vice versa. You have a partner in crime. Someone to dream with, build with, and celebrate with along the way. Even when it annoys you, the other person's presence in your life keeps your soul moving forward—it keeps the water stirred.

Marriage has been a beautiful, brilliant, God-breathed design ever since he looked down at Adam in the garden and said, "This guy is hopeless on his own." That's my paraphrase. The actual words were "It is not good for the man to be alone."[1]

Not good—even in the middle of paradise.

Adam was in the garden before the Fall, and everything was good—except for one thing. It wasn't good for him to be alone. Because as great as all the animals were, they weren't stirring the water in his soul. And stagnant water starts to stink.

So God created Eve, and marriage, and a beautiful picture of two becoming one and living happily ever after.

Which was great for them. But what about us? What about the single people in the world who don't have another person stirring the water? How do we keep our souls from turning into a stagnant swamp?

That's where we're heading. A relationship isn't a prerequisite for stirring the water. In part 1, we're going to learn how to come face-to-face with the first enemy of singleness: the past. We're going to face the pain, heal the shame, let go of yesterday, and be single today.

Chapter 1

Stagnant Water

Feel Your Feelings and Talk It Out

Is there something wrong with me?

The church parking lot had been buzzing all day, but now it was empty. Another successful Sunday. Another week of being a pastor. The sermon was done, the building was locked, the alarm was set, and all I had to do was get back to my apartment.

But I couldn't move.

For the past hour, my Chevy Cruze had been the only car left in the lot. The keys were in the ignition, but I couldn't put it in drive. I was stuck in my own head, trapped by the spiraling thoughts.

We have thousands of thoughts every day. Most come and go, but some get caught, embedding themselves in our brains, like a drill digging deeper and deeper into the earth.

Ten years ago as I sat frozen in that parking lot, one of those thoughts came.

Is there something wrong with me?

Recycled.
On repeat.
Every day.

At the time, I was a few years into being a pastor and loved it. I was working at a great church, was taking seminary classes at night, and had amazing friends. But there was one problem.

I was single.
A single pastor.

By the way, I'm still a single pastor—a much healthier one, but let's not get ahead of ourselves.

In some Christian traditions, singleness is celebrated, but that wasn't my experience. Although we've got Bible verses that say we should celebrate it, in my circles we've been pretty good at overlooking them. (Don't worry—much more on that later.)

I wasn't all that concerned about my relationship status, but everyone else sure seemed to be. My singleness was the low-hanging fruit in every service. Older guys would find me in the lobby and remind me that marriage is God's idea and that they'd really love to see me married by this time next year. And every well-intentioned aunt and grandmother was hearing from God that I was supposed to meet their niece or neighbor.

Everyone had their own method but the same message. *Time is running out. If you're single today, you should be worried about tomorrow. If you aren't searching for "the one," there must be something wrong with you. After all, you aren't getting any younger.*

The expectation was for me to be married. Or at the very least, single and ready to mingle. After all, we're here to be fruitful and multiply.[1]

Which is great.
And biblical.
And important.
And of not much interest to me.

A relationship has never been too high on my priority list. But I didn't know how to say that back then. And every time I tried, the person listening would smile as the words went in one ear and out the other, and then they'd tell me about another friend they wanted me to meet—this one was "super independent," like me.

For years, the narrative of my singleness hung around. It was the thing in the air. I'd go to work and hear it. Then I'd go to seminary and hear it again. Then during every holiday, I'd see my extended family and they'd complete the trifecta. Three strikes and you're out; you can secondhand smoke a narrative for only so long before it starts affecting you.

I say *you* because it's easier to type than *I*. But the truth is, I was laughing less, dreaming less, and sleeping less. Life was losing its luster. My soul was being buried alive underneath all the worries and confusion about my singleness—each harmless joke or comment was another handful of dirt tossed on the coffin. Until this particular Sunday night—the one that found me sitting in the parking lot—when the coffin felt six feet deep.

I was angry and upset, or at least I wanted to be. Those were the emotions I was searching for, but I couldn't find them, name them, or feel them—I didn't know I was allowed to. I couldn't even cry. I hadn't in several years. So instead, I sat in my car and stared blankly at the night sky.

That may sound a bit dramatic for the start of a book on singleness. Maybe your singleness has never kept you stuck in a parking lot. Or maybe my story feels tame compared with your experience. Whatever your story is, we've all had those moments of isolation when the loneliness sets in. Those are the moments when the first enemy of singleness (the past) can take some really cheap shots at you. Shame, regret, and pain from yesterday start telling you there's something wrong with you today.

What I really needed in that moment was for someone to teach me how to process my past (which may be the same thing you need today). I needed to talk it out. Fortunately, that week, I made one of the most important connections I've ever made.

Spiritual Direction

Bill's office smelled like lavender.

To this day, I've never seen a humidifier work harder than the one in the back corner of his small space. The incessant hum was about to escort me into new territory. The place beneath my conscious thoughts. Beneath the surface of the water, the deep end of my soul.

Once I found enough footing to put my car in drive and leave the church parking lot, I figured I should probably see a counselor. I didn't know how to do that at the time; this was before there were resources everywhere. But after a quick Google search, I found an option called spiritual direction.

Spiritual directors are basically counselors, except they are way more spiritual (that's a joke, sort of). While counselors help us work through situations in our lives and relationships, spiritual directors primarily focus on discerning what God is up to in our lives. While every director is different, sessions usually start with some Bible reading, prayer, and a little silence before you dive in and talk about whatever is going on in your life.

That sounded like a good place to start, so I sent an email to a center down the street, and a few days later, I heard back from a guy named Bill who told me he'd love to help.

I had no idea what to expect. My only experience with counseling was what I'd seen in movies, so I figured I was essentially Matt Damon from *Good Will Hunting* and would scare away the first few victims until I finally found someone who "got" me.

That's not what happened.

Mostly because I wasn't a genius with a troubled past who was running away from my potential. I was just a single pastor who was overthinking my singleness.

The counseling space was small but cozy. Besides a couple of chairs, a side table with a Bible on it was the only other piece of furniture. Bill casually sat down, waving at the other chair, inviting me to join him. He had thick, long, unkempt hair and was wearing the baggiest pants I'd ever seen, matched with an oversize plain black T-shirt and flip-flops. The same uniform he would sport every session over the next several years.

"Coffee?" he asked, raising a Styrofoam cup.

I'd been a pastor long enough to know that deep conversations are more manageable when you're sipping on a hot drink, so I nodded. And although he didn't say anything, I'm confident he noticed my shaky hand when I took the cup, coffee spilling over the top and splashing on the floor. As I would soon discover, despite his laid-back appearance, Bill was always observing. Not in a judgmental way, but rather like a fisherman watching the water patterns, or a comic studying human behavior.

"I picked out a passage for us," Bill said, his voice calm. "I'm going to read it. Then I'll be silent. Whenever you are ready, start talking."

That felt like an odd strategy.

That's it?

I came from a fast-paced pastoral job, where we made quick decisions and had so many people to meet with that we had to keep conversations swift and efficient.

But I nodded again, and the room went still.

Really still.

The only sound was the humming of the humidifier lofting lavender into the air. Which I needed because the longer we sat in silence, the louder the events of the day became. Random thoughts
kept popping up. As if my brain were taking a last stand, trying to
protect me from what waited below the surface.

That budget meeting was brutal.
I have so much to get done before my sermon on Sunday.
Maybe I shouldn't be a pastor.
Is there something wrong with me?
Oh shoot, I forgot to call Andy back.

This whole "inner work" thing was new territory for me. Taking
time to feel my feelings and talk to someone about them was outside my comfort zone. I'd gotten really good at encouraging
others to do it, but I figured it was time to practice what I
preached. As uncomfortable as it was, I knew I needed it, so I
took a breath and tried to let the hum usher me into the stillness.

Then Bill opened his Bible to the fifth chapter of John's gospel and
began to read a story about the Pool of Bethesda.

The Pool
In first-century Palestine, Jerusalem was the center of religious
activity.

Near one of the gates of Jerusalem was a pool aptly named
Bethesda (an Aramaic word that means "house of mercy"). There
was a belief passed down from generation to generation that this
pool was special; it had healing power. Most of the time, the
water was stagnant. When the water was stagnant, it was an ordinary pool. But once in a while, an angel would come down from

heaven and stir the water. When that happened, the first person
to enter the pool would be healed.[2]

As you can imagine, everyone who needed physical healing
would hang there, waiting for the angel to stir the water, including one guy who had been unable to walk for thirty-eight years.
We don't know how long he had been lying by the pool—the text
doesn't tell us—but as Bill read the story to me, I couldn't help but
speculate a little. Imagine if he had spent most (if not all) thirty-
eight years there. Some people probably came and went, checking
in whenever they passed by to see if they could get lucky. But I
wonder if this man had doubled down on this narrative. If he was
so desperate for healing that he laid down his mat and set up
shop by the water for decades.

Think about that for a second.

On day one, he was probably full of hope, waiting for his miracle.
When it didn't come, he figured day two would be his day.

But then a week went by with no results.
And then a month.
And then a year.
Then two.
Then ten.

At some point, the excitement must've worn off. You can hold on
to the hope that tomorrow might be different for only so long.
There's a limit to the amount of time you can stare. Stare at the
stagnant water long enough, and eventually you lose hope it will
ever be stirred.

That may sound like a strange story to you, and I agree. You may
be wondering if there was really an angel who flew by to stir the
water. So do I. And you're probably doubting that the first person
to enter the stirred water truly experienced healing. Fair enough.

But what I do know is that after years of trying the same strategy, hope would be hard to come by.

I pictured the man lying on his mat as his hope turned into doubt, and then eventually, that doubt gave way to apathy. There once was a day when he had believed the water would heal him, but now the water was stagnant.

My heart was speeding up as Bill read.

One of the beautiful things about the Bible is that although it's about other people, sometimes it feels like it speaks directly to us. I pictured myself sitting on my mat by that ancient pool, unable to move. But just like the Bethesda pool, the water in my soul was so stagnant that I was spending my evenings stuck in church parking lots.

That was about to change.

Bill was a master of the craft. He read the passage again, slowing down this time as the man on his mat said, "I have no one to help me into the pool when the water is stirred."[3] It's as if he knew what was going on in my soul better than I did.

"That's me," I blurted out before Bill could finish the story.

He stopped.

"Sorry," I said, silently cursing myself for interrupting and wondering if spiritual direction was something you could flunk. "I should let you finish. I've never done this before."

But he put his Bible down and smiled. Then the questions began.

Questions That Stir

"What were you feeling that night in the parking lot?" Bill asked after I told him the reason I'd reached out.

"That's the thing. . . . I don't know," I told him truthfully. "I guess that's the problem. I just felt numb—still do. My soul feels as stagnant as that pool from the story."

Intellect has always come much more naturally than emotions.

IQ—I'm doing all right.
EQ (aka emotional intelligence)—not so much.

In school, tests were easy, but navigating hallways and lunchrooms and social status was a whole different animal.

Bill nodded knowingly. "Numb counts as something," he said with a smile. (By the way, I've always held on to that line. If you're struggling to feel anything as you read the beginning of this book, remember, numb counts as something. The other emotions will come as we do some of the work in the next few chapters, but in the beginning, let yourself off the hook.)

"Let's not talk about you, then," he continued. "You're a pastor. How do you feel like we handle relationships in the church?"

"Not well," I said. "I just don't get it. It feels like everyone else is in on a joke that I don't understand."

I meant every word. It was starting to feel like the whole God thing was a front for finding love.

I told him about the number of times I've watched someone be totally invested in their faith and then just fall off the face of the earth when they get in a relationship. Or get super involved when dating someone only to disappear when they break up. *Who's the god in that equation?*

I told him how, on multiple occasions, I've been the third wheel with a couple making out in the baptismal pool after I dunked them. *Cool, cool, cool . . . I think you kinda get it.*

"Fair enough," Bill said, observing my laughter but sensing the anger beneath it. "But why do you think that all makes you so mad?"

"Because the questions and the jokes make me wonder if there's something wrong with me," I admitted unexpectedly.

That was all Bill needed. He was like Luke Skywalker flying his X-wing toward the Death Star, knowing that even the most well-guarded fortresses have a weak point. My soul may have seemed completely closed off, but all he needed was one tiny opening. He noticed that question got a visceral reaction out of me and seized his opportunity, firing questions through the tiny window and into the depths of my soul to blow everything up.

"Have you been single your whole life?"

"Yeah," I told him. "I mean, when I was twenty, I was in a relationship for a few months, but that's it."

"How'd it end?" he asked.

"Anticlimactically. She called me one night and told me, although she knew I was a laid-back person, she was feeling insecure about how casually I was taking the whole thing."

"How'd that make you feel?" Bill asked, listening intently.

"She was right. Completely justified. It's not like I wasn't trying. I just didn't have the same desire that most people seem to have to be in a romantic relationship. So, we broke up."

"And that's the extent of your dating?"

"I tried a few more times through my early twenties," I told him, feeling like we were talking about pretty silly things for a session of spiritual direction. "I went on a handful of dates and enjoyed most of them. I got rejected once or twice,[4] but most of the time, I'd get to the point where I'd be honest enough with myself to admit I'm just not all that interested in having a partner."

"Why do you think it took you so long to admit that to yourself?" he asked.

"I guess because no one else seems to think that way," I said. "And no one else seems to think I should think that way." Most single people I meet with are hoping their singleness is coming to an end, not just getting started. I knew my way of thinking was a little unusual.

"And that makes you feel . . ."

"Like there's something wrong with me," I interjected sharply, a knot beginning to tighten in my chest. *I just met this guy. He's simply asking questions. Relax.*

Bill gave me a reassuring nod, patiently prodding me to follow my anger, to let it out instead of pushing it down. "Do you want to be in a relationship?" he asked, setting up his shot.

"What I want is for everyone to leave me alone," I told him, my face red and my blood beginning to boil. "I feel like everyone else is way more concerned about my relationship status than I am."

"Do you think you are single because there is something wrong with you?"

"No!" I practically shouted, the knot in my chest bursting. "I think that's what other people think about me. But I can never seem to explain myself to people. It's like they don't get it."

The frontline soldiers in my soul, who are in charge of making sure I behave, made their last stand. I took a breath, hoping Bill would break the silence, but he didn't—I knew he wouldn't.

I was playing checkers.
Bill was playing chess.
And he put me in checkmate.

"Because Jesus was single!" I nearly yelled. "How are we not see-ing this? I feel like I'm going crazy here. Why does everyone think I'm the weird one? We talk about following the way of Jesus, except apparently with one massive exception. WWJD? Probably not get married, but no one seems to see that."

I took a breath, but Bill wouldn't let me back down. "Give it a name," he said. "What are you feeling?"

"I'm frustrated!" I said. "I don't know where we got this narrative that singleness is the enemy of holiness. All I know is we didn't get it from Scripture."

He sat back, lifting his hands, motioning for me to continue.

"How about John the Baptist?" I said. "You know, the one who prepared the way for the Messiah? I've read the Gospels many times, and I've never seen a Mrs. Baptist. Unless she was down with locusts and wild honey for dinner every night, I'm pretty sure he was on his own."

The humidifier was humming like a crowd cheering me on.

"I mean, there's Martha. I'm speculating here," I told him, for some reason feeling the need to cite my sources and explain myself to my own spiritual director. "But it seems like she was the head of her home. Which back then meant she was most likely single. And she hosted some of Jesus's most significant nights of ministry. And then there's Paul," I continued. "Ever heard of him? The one who wrote thirteen of the twenty-seven books of the New Testament, planted like fourteen churches, and took the gospel farther than anyone before him. And he managed to do it all as a single person. So, Bill, if you are keeping score," I said, reaching the crescendo of my rant, "that means the one who paved the way for the Savior of the world, the one who hosted the Savior of the world, the one who took the Savior of the world's message to the ends of the earth—and, by the way, the Savior of the world— are on a long list of people who didn't wait until they were married to begin their ministry. And so, yes, I'm frustrated," I said, standing now. "I have no idea why no one else sees this. Please tell me you do."

Bill was smiling; he knew we were getting somewhere. I was feeling my feelings. I was talking it out—the water in my soul was stirring.

What About You?
Remember what happened to my neighborhood pool when Jeff and Judy stopped showing up to stir the water? That's how my soul felt until Bill started asking me the right questions.

Do you ever feel stuck in a rut? Like each day is turning into a slightly less exciting rerun of the day before? Like someone is turning down the saturation and the vivid colors of the world are fading to shades of gray? Ever feel like laughter is getting harder and harder to come by? Ever feel like the good gift of a glass of wine with friends is slowly turning into a prerequisite for being present? Ever feel like you used to have creative ideas and big dreams for your future but now you're just trying to get through the day? Is an unhealthy pattern in your life starting to feel permanent? Ever feel your lust for life fading?

Those are symptoms of stagnant water. Those were *my* symptoms of a stagnant soul.

That's what your past can do to you. Oftentimes, when you feel stuck in the present, it's because you haven't dealt with the pain in your past. You begin to lose your passion for today because you can't stop replaying and ruminating on yesterday.

For all its beauty, life beats you up as you go. People betray you, lie to you, reject you, and gossip about you (and you return the favor). You get some lucky breaks, and you get some unlucky ones. Sometimes there's a drought when you need it to rain, and other times there's a downpour on your wedding day. In one hospital room, there are tears of joy, and in the next one, the tears hold deep pain.

Life is breathtakingly beautiful and callously cruel all at the same time. You aren't a blank slate every morning; today isn't immune to yesterday. When left untouched and unprocessed, that pain can keep you stuck on your mat, especially when you're single.

It's the classic Hollywood trope.

Boy meets girl, falls in love, and gets his life in order. Then she breaks his heart and he shuts down. Plops down on the couch on a Friday and watches the extended cut of the entire *Lord of the Rings* trilogy on repeat until the next Friday. Cut to Friday number three, and he's still there. The only thing that's changed is that his beard is longer and his breath is sharper—the apartment around him getting progressively dirtier as plates pile up in the sink. By the fourth Friday, he smells so bad that his dog takes one whiff and walks away. "What?" he calls out as the dog scurries away. "Now you're going to leave me too?"

Fade to black.

The rushing water in his soul has gone stagnant. Several bowls of ice cream and interviews with Peter Jackson about how they filmed the Battle of Helm's Deep later, that stagnant water stinks. Our poor protagonist can't enjoy being single today because he's still caught up in yesterday.

Right around that time, there's a knock on the door. Enter the mentor who is going to stir the water again. He throws open the blinds, and lights flood into the apartment, revealing it's the middle of the afternoon. The protagonist winces at the light, and despite his protest, the mentor turns off the TV, pulls him off the couch, and pushes him back into the real world.

Don't worry. The rest of this book won't be cliché movie scenes, but the thing about Hollywood tropes is that they are littered with truth. Exaggerated truth. But truth nonetheless. We spend seventeen dollars on a ticket (which isn't nearly as bad as all those in a relationship who have to spend thirty-four dollars) and sit through a two-hour movie because, deep down, it's speaking truth about us.

This particular trope hits close to home for me. I know the single space really well; I've lived in it my entire life. The space where you can decide to be completely selfish with your time if you choose. Where you can think about yourself all day if you want. Where you can watch the *Lord of the Rings* trilogy all the way through, posting a picture between movies two and three to keep up appearances, and lock yourself away like Bilbo Baggins in Bag End[5] for an entire day (just as an example).

No one sets out to live that way, but then life happens. The cruel parts aren't easily forgotten. We carry the pain and shame from difficult moments around with us, like an overzealous packer trudging through the airport.

Get bogged down by enough baggage, and soon enough, you realize it's a lot easier to just lie down on your mat and wait for someone to carry you. It's easier to stare at the stagnant water and blame the absent angel who doesn't seem to be doing their part.

Your soul stops thriving and starts merely surviving.

It gets stagnant. It gets stuck—trapped in yesterday instead of taking on today.

If I'm talking to you, I've got some really good news. When you keep reading in the gospel of John, you'll notice that Jesus specializes in stirring stagnant water. He didn't just heal the guy who had been on his mat for thirty-eight years; he walked into a festival, looked out over a sea of stagnant souls, and declared, "Let anyone who is thirsty come to me and drink. Whoever believes in me, as Scripture has said, rivers of living water will flow from within them."[6]

Your soul may feel like a stagnant swamp, but it's meant to be a river of living water. Swamps stink, but rivers refresh. They sustain. They move life forward. You're made to do the same. Jesus gave us all an invitation to break down the dam and turn the stagnant swamp into a rushing river.

If you feel like I did that night in the church parking lot, you're not alone. Unpacking your past isn't easy; it can be hard to even know where to start. But the starting point for Jesus, Bill, and all the other mentors I've had in my life seems to always be just asking good questions, so here goes:

Is there something about singleness that irritates you?

Is there a part of this topic that makes you want to go on a rant?

Did I say something in this chapter that frustrated you?

Don't rush this process. You can't heal what you can't feel. If you're anything like me, there may be a voice in your head telling you emotions like anger are bad and should be ignored. But that's not true. Anger can actually be an ally. Annoyance and irritation are like breadcrumbs leading you to the deeper parts of yourself; following them is the best way to stir the water in your soul.

So, follow them by writing out your answers to these questions in a journal or calling a trusted friend to vent about them.

Following the feelings and being honest about where they came from is the first step to healing, but as we'll talk about in the next chapter, that's just the beginning.

Chapter 2

The Ones That Got Away

Give It a Name, Give It Some Space, Let It Go

The first time I ever danced with a girl was homecoming, my freshman year of high school. I had no idea what I was doing.

My friends and I walked into the dance hall (which was just our cafeteria with the overhead lights off and streamers on the walls). The strobe lights, haze, and loud music were enough to distract us from the smell of leftover pizza that wafted through that cafeteria 24/7—super romantic.

There was a girl across the cafeteria named Jamie. She was with her friends; I was with mine. Everything was fine until a slow song came on and kids started pairing up left and right. The pool of potential partners shrank quickly, and I realized with dread that if I didn't make a move, I would be against the wall, pretending to care about the streamers for the next three and a half minutes.

But then I caught Jamie's eye. She smiled. I smiled back. And I'm not sure if it was the punch, the streamers, the pizza, or the fact that she didn't want to be the last one standing without a partner either, but ten seconds later, we were dancing together.

This was a new experience for me; I wasn't quite sure what to do. I knew Jamie from history class, so I thought about asking her about the Revolutionary War, but I didn't know if academic small talk was standard protocol for a dance. So instead, I just took a few deep breaths, smiled, and did my best to avoid stepping on her toes.

Everything was fine. I was present. I was alive. I was dancing with Jamie. Until I started listening to the lyrics. This was no fun, up-beat, probably-inappropriate-for-a-high-school-cafeteria song. This one was romantic—"Amazed" by Lonestar. A love song about two people who are head over heels for each other, but Jamie was just some girl I sat next to in history class. As it reached the first chorus, I realized I had made a terrible mistake:

> *I wanna spend the rest of my life*
> *With you by my side*
> *Forever and ever*[1]

Suddenly, the walls started closing in, and we were slow dancing in a burning room.

Wait. What? No, I just sit next to this girl in history class. I just didn't want to be the last person without a dance partner. I didn't know that's what this was . . .

I'm sure she could tell how tense my fourteen-year-old body was getting as I started rehearsing an exit speech:

Look, Jamie, I think you're great. It's just that forever and ever is an awfully long time. Plus, my band has a show at a coffee shop on Wednesday. . . . Well, actually, it's an open mic night, but we've got this new song, and it could be our big break, so I'll probably be on the road a lot for our summer tour, and this just wouldn't be fair to you. It's not you; it's me. And I know everyone always says that, but I really mean it. Thanks so much for dancing, but if you'll excuse me, I'm just going to take off at a dead sprint down the street into the night and not stop until I see the sunrise.

In other words . . . I panicked.

Because of a sappy song at a silly dance.

Was that logical? Of course not. Jamie didn't think I was proposing. She was just enjoying (or trying to enjoy) a dance at homecoming. Today I can see that, but I couldn't for a long time.
Instead, I stuffed that memory down into some deep recess of my
soul—stuck it in the corner and tried to forget about it—for years.
Every once in a while, it'd pop out of the corner it was hiding in,
hijacking me in the present moment and dragging me back into
an awkward memory that always left me wondering where the
panic came from.

Do you have any moments like that? Any awkward encounters,
humiliating situations, or just uncomfortable memories that you
try to stuff down and ignore? Since you're a human, I'm going to
assume the answer is yes. The better question is, Is it possible to
heal those memories?

I didn't know the answer to that question until years later when I
made up a game with my friends called The Ones That Got Away.
Let me explain . . .

The Game

After high school was college, and then after college, I traveled
the world for a year with three of my best friends—Doug (my
brother), Ethan, and Matt. We started in Haiti and just kept heading west until we ended up back in the United States. Along the
way, we lived with local pastors, helping them with whatever they
needed, learning their strategies for church, experiencing other
cultures, eating a lot of different food, and living life.

The year was packed full of adventures—one of the best years of
my life. But there was also a lot of in-between time. Have you

ever noticed how you always remember the highlights of travel—
the weekends and the waterfalls—but you forget just how much
waiting is involved?

Waiting for planes.
Waiting for trains.
Waiting for automobiles.

Traveling requires a lot of patience, especially when you don't
have a phone. We didn't have any phones with us the entire year.
That sounds insane today as I write it, but that was part of the adventure. We wanted to be completely unplugged. You know that
feeling you get when you're waiting in line at the grocery store
and your phone dies, which means you have to stand there for
five minutes with nothing to do? We had a year of that. Hours
and hours of downtime to fill.

I should also point out that we had just graduated college. We had
been roommates at the University of Colorado Boulder and had
one of those houses where the door was not just always unlocked
but literally always open. (As in, we never took the time to close
the door.) Everyone knew they had an open invitation into our
home. Collectively, we hung out with hundreds of people during
college. But suddenly, it was just the four of us. As you can imagine, when we went from being around hundreds of friends to
traveling with three other guys and really not seeing any girls at
all, it didn't take long for us to go crazy.

So we created a game called The Ones That Got Away.

The rules were simple: Each of us came with a list of names, including every potential love interest we could think of from the
past. Our lists were full of breakups and rejections, things we'd
said but wished we hadn't, and things we hadn't said but wished
we had. It didn't matter if it was a two-year relationship or a two-

minute rejection. A gut-wrenching heartbreak or a story about panicking in a cafeteria because of some lyrics. If there was an anecdote, we wanted to hear it.

We dug deep, recalling every story we could drum up. Every moment that had been sitting down in the dungeons of our souls finally got to see the light of day. And now you're thinking, *That must've taken forever.* Yep. It's amazing what you find when you start digging. But remember, we had a lot of time and few ways to fill it. The Ones That Got Away became our entertainment for the year.

We'd look forward to the downtime all day. Whoever was next up in the rotation picked from their list the name of a girl from their past and told us the tale (or saga). Most of the time, the stories would be full of laughter (nothing new for us), but then, occasionally, we'd start feeling other emotions like sadness, confusion, relief, or regret (something brand new for us).

Sometimes jokes turned into tears.
Other times tears turned into jokes.
Sometimes the storyteller started crafting an apology letter.
Other times the storyteller would turn on some Garth Brooks and start thanking God for unanswered prayers.[2]

All valid responses that wouldn't have happened if we hadn't played the game—if we hadn't taken our greatest insecurities, the ones we'd buried deep in the earth, and brought them back up to the surface.

That's how memories work. Especially the difficult, sad, embarrassing, or downright awkward ones. I have plenty; I'm sure you have some too. They love the dark. They linger in the shadows. And they only ever make an appearance to mess up a perfectly good moment by reminding you they are still there.

Until we shine a light.
Until we talk about them.
Until we tell people we trust about them.

The Jamie story was just one example—a fairly easy one. In the dark, it was a traumatic story about panic and pain. In the light, it became a humorous tale about a kid who was prone to overthinking.

That memory used to make me shudder and shut down. Now I think it's hilarious. All because I talked it out with people I trusted.

We didn't understand what was happening at the time; all we knew was that a mindless game we'd invented was turning into one of the most life-giving exercises we'd ever done. It wasn't until years later, when I sat in Bill's office telling him about the game, that I discovered some language for what was actually going on.

Wells

Lavender wafted through Bill's office again. At this point, I was used to the smell. I expected it. We were several sessions in, none quite as climactic as the first. But on this particular day, I was about to discover my next step to being single today.

The story he read was from John's gospel again. It was one chapter before the man and his mat. This one was about a woman at a well.[3]

The middle of the day was the worst time to fetch water from the well. Pulling water out of the earth was exhausting enough; add the scorching sun, and it became excruciating.

But she preferred it that way. The sun didn't burn nearly as bad as the stares she got from the other women in the early hours of the day. It had been that way ever since her first marriage ended. The second failed marriage didn't help, and the third only made it worse.

Judgmental looks.
Passive-aggressive comments.
Eventually, she opted for the heat of the day over the fervor of the gossip.

She'd fetch water at noon, and no one would ever be the wiser. When she reached the well at midday, she wasn't expecting to run into anyone, much less a Jewish rabbi.

Jesus primarily split his time between two regions—Galilee (northern Israel) and Judea (southern Israel). He seemed to prefer being up north in Galilee, where he grew up. However, Jerusalem (where all the action was) was in Judea. So Jesus and his disciples frequently made the trip from Galilee to Judea.

This is significant because there was a region right in the middle of the two called Samaria.

The Samaritans got a bad rap in those days. A Jew walking into Samaria was like a Yankees fan walking into Fenway Park. But that's exactly what Jesus did. In John 4, he brought his disciples through Samaria, and after walking all morning, he got tired and sat down by a well.

A few moments later, the Samaritan woman showed up to draw water.

Unlike me, who got my water straight from the faucet this morning, they had to get their water from streams, rivers, and lakes. And when there wasn't a body of water nearby, they had to dig down to find it. There's an immense amount of water under us, but it's covered by layers of dirt and rock.

That's a good picture of the human soul, isn't it? The running water (joy, hope, and zeal for life) is down there somewhere, but it gets covered beneath layers of pain, embarrassment, and confusion. Bury it deep enough and you forget that it's down there. That's certainly been true for me, and as we're about to find out, it was also true for the woman Jesus encountered at the well.

It didn't take him long to start digging into the woman's story.

"I don't have a husband," she told Jesus at one point in the conversation.

"Well, you've had five, haven't you? And the guy you're with now isn't one of them, right?"

Wait. What?

Jesus was playing the original game of The Ones That Got Away. He just called out her greatest insecurity, the one she'd buried deep in the shadows. The shame that kept her responses short. The pain that kept her visiting the well in the middle of the day.

She wanted to cover up her past, but Jesus wasn't interested in letting her stay stuck in that shame. So, he named it. All of it. All five guys from her past and the sixth that seemed to be heading in that direction: The Ones That Got Away. He was reminding her that her past didn't disqualify her.

He helped her reach into the depths of her soul, the place where the rushing water was buried by fear, anger, and shame.

She got defensive at first, then embarrassed, and then set free. The more time she spent with Jesus, the freer she felt. That deep stream, dammed up by years of guilt and shame, became a river of living water. Thanks to an unlikely friend willing to sit and talk.

By the end of the conversation, she was running back to town to tell everyone about Jesus.

I'd heard that story a hundred times, but as Bill read, I felt like I was hearing it for the first time. I told him about playing The Ones That Got Away a few years earlier and how much freedom I'd felt when I finally had time to process my past.

More importantly, I told him I hadn't done anything like that since. "When I got back from that trip, I started working at a church. I became a pastor. A professional Christian."

That was the moment I stopped confronting my past.

I'm a pastor now. I can't be talking about all that stuff from yesterday. People are counting on me today.

No one taught me that narrative; I just picked it up along the way. I started meeting with people every day, helping them walk through the tough stuff in their lives, and stopped even glancing at my own stuff.

If they asked about me, I'd say something generic.

If pressed, I'd get short.
If pressed further, I'd get mad.
If pressed from there, I'd shut down.

In the name of leadership.

Ironically, all the great leaders in my life were saying the opposite thing. I'd hear Craig Groeschel say, "People would rather follow a leader who is always real than one who is always right."[4]

Yeah! That's good, Craig. Let me write that one down for the fifth time in my journal.

On paper, I couldn't agree more.
In practice, I couldn't agree less.

My Moleskine journal was packed full of one-liners from leaders urging me to be real, but there was a voice in my head telling me to pretend like I was always right. Where did it get me?

Stuck in a church parking lot.
Car in park.
Emotions in park.
Life in park.

As lavender spewed out of the humidifier, all those emotions spewed out of my soul. I told Bill how much I missed feeling free to process, free to admit weakness, free to not be okay, and he just sat there listening patiently.

"Give it a name. Give it some space. And let it go," he said when I was done.

"I'm sorry," I responded. "What do you mean?"

"Being real is what you guys were doing on your trip. That's what Jesus did in the story . . ."

"And that's what I'm missing in my life right now," I blurted out, saying what he wouldn't. We both knew it was true, but he always let me come to my own conclusions. "Ever since I went pro," I added with more than a hint of sarcasm.

Bill continued, "Until you talk about it, that water stays stagnant. It sits there, unnoticed, like water from a leaky pipe sitting behind some drywall. You have no idea that it's there, but it's slowly destroying your house."

All right, take it easy, Bill.

"Talking it out stirs the water," he said calmly. "Give it a name, give it some space, and then learn the lost art of letting it go."

How to Stir

Today is a gift. But single people often have a hard time unwrapping and enjoying it because we have too much unprocessed pain from our past dragging us back down into the abyss. If that's you, the good news is, it doesn't have to be that way; we can take a play out of Bill's playbook.

Give it a name.
Give it some space.
Let it go.

Three simple steps that will start to stir the stagnant water in your soul. Let's unpack them.

Give It a Name

"I feel like a kid," I told Keith one day while we were eating lunch. Keith is a friend of mine who shares a love for telling stories. We were meeting to talk about a podcast we were going to start called *Stories in Scripture,* where we—wait for it—tell stories in Scripture.

But then the conversation turned, and I began telling Keith about my sessions with Bill.

"All the spiritual stuff has always come naturally to me," I told him. "And I can hang in most intellectual circles. But it's my emotions—I can't even figure out how I'm feeling."

Keith just laughed. We're cut from the same cloth. We love to use our minds, but using our hearts takes some work. He has an incredible wife and awesome kids who have pushed him to put in a lot of that work.

As God once noted, "It is not good for the man to be alone."[5]

"Do you know what I had to do at first?" Keith said, gearing up to give me some of the simplest but most brilliant advice I've ever gotten. (Isn't it funny how those two things tend to go hand in hand?) "This is sort of embarrassing, but I had to carry a list of emotions with me."

"Really?"

"Yeah, like an NFL quarterback checking their cheat sheet for the play in the huddle," he said. "I would just work my way down the list one word at a time and ask myself if I felt that way. And when I found it, I'd say it out loud: 'I feel confused. I feel upset.'"

"You can do that?" I asked.

"What?"

"I mean, that's brilliant. Can you send me that list?" I asked as if it were some top-secret document only people with a security clearance could get their hands on.

Keith smiled, deciding to hold back on the joke he wanted to make about how I could google it and thousands of viable options (like an emotion wheel) would show up. "Of course."

He'd discovered something essential about confronting the past: There is power in naming things. That's why new parents give their kid a name when they introduce them to the world. The social media post is powerful because we learn the name. Imagine a caption that just said, "This is our child." Hardly the same effect.

It's like those volcanoes we made as kids. The chemical compound in the volcano would sit dormant until we added the vinegar. Then the chemicals would react, and we'd cheer.

Giving your pain a name is like adding vinegar.

That's why four guys sitting on a train traveling through India could have such a profound experience talking about the ones that got away. The pain might have always been there, sitting dormant, but the moment you give it a name, watch what happens.

If you're single and trying to live like Jesus, you will face (and likely already have faced) a unique set of challenges. The struggles of singleness are real, and since we don't always talk about them, it's easy to let them accumulate and compound. The only way forward is to confront your past by learning to name the things that happened and the emotions that accompanied those experiences.

Even if that means that you, like me, need to start by printing out a list of emotions and practicing naming them. The way I see it, if Tom Brady can take a cheat sheet into the huddle, I can carry around a list of emotions in my pocket.

And if you want to make fun of me for that, well, guess what? That makes me feel—hold on; give me a second to scan— *indifferent*.

Give It Some Space
Do you remember DVDs?

If you don't, I'll catch you up. Before all the streaming services, movies were actual items you could hold in your hand. DVDs came out in 1997 and were a huge improvement on the VHS.

DVDs were a game changer. Unlike a VHS, they broke movies up into scenes and allowed you to skip right to the part you wanted instead of having to rewind, fast-forward, rewind, and then fast-forward one more time.

Which was phenomenal.
Until it wasn't.

As someone smarter than me once said, "Every rose has its thorn." The internet is a gift—until it gives hackers access to your information. Making money is amazing—until it drives you mad. And DVDs were great—until they got a tiny little scratch. One scratch was all it took for the movie to get stuck on a scene.

Immediately after Gandalf took his stand against the Balrog to buy Frodo enough time to escape and is about to fall into the abyss, the scene starts to skip.

"Fly, you fools—"
"Fly, you f—"
"Fl—"

Right back to the beginning of the scene. Did Gandalf survive? Did Frodo and the Fellowship escape? Did they heed Gandalf's wish and fly to Mordor instead of walking? I'll tell you the answer to at least one of those questions is no.[6]

Why does this guy keep bringing up The Lord of the Rings? *I think that trope from the last chapter was autobiographical.*

The DVD had a lethal flaw—skipping, freezing, and then replaying the same old scene.

And that, I realized in Bill's office, is hauntingly similar to how my mind works. Pain and shame from the past are like scratches on a DVD. I try so hard to move forward, but then a scene from my past pops up and plays again.

And again.
And again.
And again.

I don't think that person ever liked me.
I don't know why.
I've only ever been nice to them.
Must be their thing.
Yeah, their thing for sure—nothing to do with me.

Just this morning, I played this exact monologue in my head. I was on a walk, thinking through this chapter. The streets were quiet, and the birds were chirping, the brisk fall air such a relief after a long, hot Austin summer. It was a great moment.

And then it got hijacked out of nowhere, and I started thinking about a person I hadn't even seen in two years. Skip, skip, stuck. My DVD got stuck on a scene from the past.

I bet you know the feeling.

And let's be honest—when it comes to romantic relationships from the past, the intensity of this phenomenon is cranked up even higher. Those awkward, uncomfortable, or upsetting scenes get caught on a loop.

Here's some tough love: For as long as you refuse to not just name that memory and the emotions but create space to feel them, that scratch will remain on your DVD. Spoiling moments today by re-playing scenes from yesterday.

I think The Ones That Got Away worked so well because we took our time with the stories. We entered into the memories and gave ourselves space to feel them. That fixes the scratch on the DVD. That painful moment from the past becomes just another scene you can move past instead of an obsession.

Not to speculate too much about the woman at the well, but it sure seems like she had some scenes she was stuck on, doesn't it? After all, the text tells us she'd had five different husbands throughout her life.[7] Have you ever thought about how difficult that must've been? How much pain she must've accumulated from that pattern of attaching and detaching? Maybe some embarrassment. Some confusion. Some resentment. Some moments she was stuck replaying.

I use the woman at the well as an example because it's easier than talking about myself. And I use that example of me trying to dance with Jamie in the cafeteria because the stakes were pretty low and it's easier to talk about that one than some others. But we all have those scenes from the past, and the trick is to give them space.

Is it any wonder it's such a struggle to stay present today? Is it any wonder singleness feels more like a curse to endure than a gift to enjoy? More like a burden than a blessing?

Over the years, my friend Shannon has taught me a lot about how to give those moments space. We've been good friends for a long time, and a lot of our mutual friends got married a decade ago. So, at every party, there's the married people and then there's us. We've had a long time to laugh about our singleness together.

"What's the biggest difference between how you approach being single in your thirties versus how you approached it in your twenties?" I asked her.

Shannon's a therapist who primarily works to help people out of drug addictions, so she's well acquainted with a lot of the deep inner work. "Probably the way I approach grief," she said contemplatively. "When you want something like marriage or kids and you don't have it, it's hard. You carry a lot of grief. Back then, I'd just fill my life with more things and ignore the grief. I don't do that anymore. I give myself space to feel it."

That got me. You've probably pieced this together by now, but panicking during an innocent dance in a high school cafeteria is a symptom of a bigger issue—a fear of commitment. Today singleness is a choice; back then, I didn't really have a say in it. I wasn't ready to be in a relationship even if I'd wanted to be. Meaning I missed out on a lot of the beauty, fun, and memories from young love. But instead of giving myself space to grieve losses like that the way my friend Shannon does, I often try to just ignore them and hope I get over them.

Is there something from the past you need to grieve? Maybe you thought a relationship was going to work out, but then it ended. Have you given yourself space to mourn? Or maybe you took a big risk and asked someone out, only to find out they didn't feel the same way. Rejection hurts. Have you given yourself space to be honest about it? Or maybe it's the frustration you feel when all your family members put pressure on you to get in a relationship. Even though you want to be in one, the right person hasn't come around yet. So now you're upset about being single and feel like you're letting your family down at the same time. That's really painful. I'm sorry you're going through that. Have you given yourself room to grieve it?

Give it a name.

Then give it some space.

If you've been divorced or widowed, you know this better than anyone else. Your yesterday may be full of pain. Or regret. Or anger. Or confusion. It's likely some combination of all of those. Being single again when you didn't expect it must be disorienting. Finding that space to grieve is going to be an essential part of your journey.

Friends can be incredibly helpful for this step, so lean on them. Call up a trusted friend, and offer to buy them a coffee if they'd be willing to just listen and create some space for you to grieve. By the way, if they're single, they probably need space, too, so offer to do the same for them.

Being single today is tough, so we have to put in the work. We have to take time to name and grieve the regret, shame, heart-break, rejection, parental pressure, and bitterness constantly trying to pull us down like the Balrog pulling Gandalf into the abyss. (Okay, enough is enough. That'll be the last *Lord of the Rings* reference for the rest of the book, I promise.)

You Shall Not Pass
I'm no therapist, just a single pastor who once made up a game with his buddies and found a lot of freedom from it. I don't know much, but I do know that, with a little work, you really can heal from things in your past. Or at least make some semblance of peace with them.

But you can heal only what you're willing to confront. You can't just draw a line, scream "You shall not pass," and expect those painful memories to go away forever. If you do, the wounds will just crawl back to their cave and gladly wreak havoc on your life.

The name of the game is to be honest about what really happened and how it made you feel. It's only after you give it a name and give it some space that you'll naturally begin to let it go.

Or in the words of Jesus, "The truth will set you free."[8]

Think about Jesus's life. When he saw outcasts, the ones who were ignored (the blind, the lame, lepers, tax collectors, and sinners), he always made room for them.

He'd sit with them.
Give them space to process.
And remind them they belonged.

Sometimes we treat difficult memories like outcasts. We don't want to be associated with them. We don't want to be seen with them. So, we draw a strict line and forbid them from passing it. We lock them away. We try to forget about them.

The longer we ignore painful memories, the more they stack up in our souls, until digging a deep well becomes the only way to access that living water buried in the ground.

The great news is, talking it out goes a long way.

As single people, we don't automatically have a person built into our lives to talk with, but when we take time to find someone (a trusted friend or a paid professional) and we get honest with them, healing is possible. When we start confronting our yesterday, it gets a lot easier to be single today.

Your past will always be part of your story, but you don't have to let it drive.

Maybe that's one of the reasons people experienced so much freedom when they encountered Jesus. Yes, he healed them, but first he usually invited them to confront the pain from their past. He sat down at a well with them and taught them how to give it a name, give it some space, and let it go.

Hopefully, you're starting to see that healing from yesterday is actually possible. The more work you put in to confront your past, the more freedom you'll begin to feel in the present.

We've covered a lot of ground so far, but when it comes to addressing the past, there's one topic that carries a unique amount of weight—so in the next chapter, we'll be talking about sex.

Chapter 3

Sex, Shame, and Stoners

Find Out What You're Medicating

"You're not quitting." My brother's voice, calm but confident, flowed through the Bluetooth in my Chevy Cruze.

"Yeah, I am," I told him again. I was about eight months into my sessions with Bill and was learning how to name the emotions I was feeling, and Doug was getting the brunt of it. "I'm out, man. I'm calling the team right now to let them know. This whole ministry thing isn't for me."

That wasn't the first time Doug had heard me say that (and it wouldn't be the last). But this one came with a time crunch. I was on my way to preach a Sunday night service at a different church and felt like the last person who should be up on a stage. I'd watched pornography less than twenty-four hours earlier, a habit I didn't want in my life but didn't know how to get rid of, and the shame was making me feel completely disqualified.

That feeling was nothing new for me.

I saw porn for the first time when I was twelve years old. Then a few years later, I watched it again. And again. It never felt right. I never walked away feeling like it was time well spent, but no matter how many times I vowed never to go back, I did.

Through a series of events in college, I started taking my faith seriously and found a lot of freedom. The vice lost its appeal for years. Like any drug, you crave it most when you're in the middle of using it. Take enough steps out, and you start to see what it really is—a twisting of a beautiful gift.

Then I became a "professional Christian." Someone who got paid to have God figured out. To explain an infinite God even though I was twenty-three. As laughable as that idea is to me today, in the middle of it, I actually believed that about myself.

Which is a lot of pressure. A lot of weight.

Eventually, I started wanting an escape again. (You know where this is heading.) I'd fight it for months, and then every once in a while, it'd find its way back into my life. The night before that phone call with my brother was one of those moments for me.

I'd been preparing for my sermon all week.
Thinking.
Reading.
Praying.
Fighting.

By the time Saturday night rolled around, I was feeling exhausted, lonely, and desperate for an escape.

Some people take shots; others go shopping.
Some people search for gummy bears; others choose gaming.
Some people reach for pills; others go to porn.

Porn was my drug of choice, and since my self-imposed title of "professional Christian" didn't allow me to make mistakes, shame was its dance partner.

I should stop here and address the obvious. I'm a pastor, not a doctor. I know porn isn't technically a drug, but over the years, I've found that language helpful. I call porn a drug as a reminder that it isn't just some harmless vice to gloss over. One of the resources I've found helpful is a website called Fight the New Drug. Here's what they have to say about it: "At a certain point, a direct comparison between the effects of drugs and the effects of porn starts to break down. . . . But at its core, if you understand the basic science of how addiction works, addiction to tobacco and addiction to pornography consumption are remarkably similar."[1]

The shame was shouting, and I was stuffing a pillow over its head, trying to silence it long enough to get through this sermon. The thought of getting up onstage, as the lights went down and every eye turned to me, made me feel like a hypocrite. *Why would I try to lead them when I can't even lead myself?*

The cognitive dissonance reverberated in my mind like nails on a chalkboard.

Hence, the full-on "break glass in case of emergency" level phone call to my brother.

"My exit is coming up," I told him. "I'm not getting off. I'm just going to keep driving right past the church and not stop driving until I get to a new state, where no one knows my name, where I can have a fresh start."

"Get off at your exit, bro."

"Maybe I'll get into real estate," I told Doug. "I feel like I'd be good at that."

"You would be, and you can look into it tomorrow. But you're preaching tonight."

"I can't talk to people about Jesus tonight. My life is a mess."

"Oh, yeah," he said with a hint of sarcasm. "You mean, like every other person who has ever tried to talk to people about Jesus?"

"I just can't do it. I feel terrible. I need . . . I need . . ."

"A Savior?" he said calmly.

He wasn't talking into a mic, but if he had been, he could've dropped it. I was getting up onstage to talk about a God who so loved the world that he came to save us from our sin. Meanwhile, I felt like the one who had outsinned God's ability to save. Sometimes grace can be a lot easier to believe for other people than for yourself.

As I reflect on that conversation I had with my brother, it makes me smile. I wasn't really going to quit, but in the moment, I sure wanted to. That's what shame does. It takes our mistakes from the past and tries to convince us they disqualify us in the present.

Can you relate to that? Sexual immorality takes on lots of forms, but they all lead to the same lonely feeling. Has a sexual mistake of any type ever made you feel isolated, unlovable, or unqualified? If so, you know how important it is to have people you can talk to in those moments. When you start listening to the lies, you need people who will remind you about the truth.

The truth about sex is it's a beautiful, God-crafted gift. From the moment God put Adam and Eve in the garden, he told them to be fruitful and multiply.[2] It's also really easy to pervert. Porn is just one example.

Maybe you resonate with the beginning of this chapter because you gravitate toward porn too. If that's you, you're not alone. In a recent study, 91.5 percent of men and 60.2 percent of women said they had consumed pornography in the last month.[3] Or maybe for you it's hookup culture. You know a one-night stand isn't going to fulfill you the way you wish it would, but you find your-self seeking out another one. Maybe you want to be in a commit-ted, monogamous relationship, but a part of you is drawn to breaking that commitment. Maybe unfaithfulness is the reason your last relationship ended, and now this topic brings up a whole lot of fear or shame for you. We all have our own journey, but whenever we twist God's design to fit our own desires, we end up feeling shame, and when sex is involved, it takes that shame to a whole different level.

Sex is a God-given gift for deep connection,[4] but it can easily be manipulated for cheap, counterfeit connections. So, we need to talk about it. Especially in a book about being single today, be-cause few things keep us stuck in the past, reliving regret, spiral-ing in a cycle of shame, more than sex.

But first, a balancing statement. I'm writing this book about sin-gleness from my worldview as a follower of Jesus—meaning that although I'm going to constantly fall short, my goal in life is to try to live like Jesus. If you don't subscribe to that belief, I'm so glad you're reading this book, because there's a lot you can get out of it. But you'll probably disagree with a lot of what I say in this chapter. I'd love it if you read it, even if you disagree with what I say. After all, conversation is how we move forward. But if you don't want my perspective, here's the skip button:

Skip

Consider this my personal invitation to head to chapter 4. That one is about Disney World; you're going to love it. I'll see you there.

If you want to keep reading this chapter, now's a good time to talk about Jesus.

Single like Jesus

Jesus was single—have I mentioned that yet?—which means we have a guide, a Jedi, a guru. Or in Jewish terms, a rabbi.

In the first century, rabbis would offer up an invitation with two words: "Follow me." This translates to "Go everywhere I go. Do everything I do. Learn to live like me." It was an invitation not just to watch and marvel at your rabbi but to practice living like him, to go and do likewise.

The person following the rabbi was his disciple, and in Matthew 28, Jesus told his disciples to go make disciples all across the world.[5] In other words, each of us has the invitation to follow Jesus. To learn to talk like Jesus, walk like Jesus, and love like Jesus.

To be a disciple.

Waking up every morning with the goal of living like Jesus infuses so much purpose into your life. But it also means you do your best to let your rabbi's beliefs shape yours, not the other way around.

As a disciple, the best place to begin a conversation about sex is to go back to what Jesus had to say about it. When you do that honestly, you realize he had a pretty strict sexual ethic:

> You have heard that it was said, "You shall not commit adultery." But I tell you that anyone who looks at a woman lustfully has already committed adultery with her in his heart.[6]

> If your right eye causes you to stumble, gouge it out and throw it away.[7]

> Haven't you read . . . "For this reason a man will leave his father and mother and be united to his wife, and the two will

become one flesh"? So they are no longer two, but one flesh. Therefore what God has joined together, let no one separate.[8]

To Jesus, sex was reserved for the covenant of marriage. Two people committing to each other emotionally, mentally, and financially—then physically.

Which is great for that happy couple on their honeymoon. But what about us? What does that truth mean for you and me as single people?

Well, the church has been trying to answer that question for thousands of years. And we haven't done a good job. For most of the journey, the church has opted to heap shame on the subject instead of diving into the depths of it.

Around the time Doug convinced me not to quit, I went and visited a different church with a friend of mine, and the pastor was talking about singleness. It was the first time I'd ever heard that topic discussed in the church, and I was really excited.

The strange part was that the pastor was married and had been since he was young. I appreciated everything he said and truly thought it was great that he was entering that space with us. I agreed with everything he said about Jesus's sexual ethic, but something felt off. Like he was rushing through a list of things not to do so he could say "Amen" and then go have sex with his spouse without giving it—or us—another thought.

It almost made sex feel like a bait and switch. Like a trick to get a couple to read their vows and lock in forever. I'm the opposite of a marriage expert, but that doesn't seem to me like a great reason to get hitched.

And underneath that, there was this feeling that sex drive is something that can't be controlled. As if it's burning like a wildfire. Worse, sometimes we talk about sex like it's oxygen. *You can go without it for a bit, but the clock is ticking. . . . Eventually, you're going to get light-headed, pass out, and die.*

Except that's not true.

When we approach sex like it's an unavoidable evil, we end up walking around full of fear on the days we're able to resist sexual temptation and shame on the days we fall into it. Neither fear nor shame is fertile ground for healthy and helpful conversations because they both refuse to dive into the depths and explore what is really going on beneath the surface.

Fear and shame distort the fact that sex is a good gift from a good God. They (fear and shame) make dirty something God deems holy. They idolize sex, making the wrong use of it, rather than redeeming it or pointing people to its beautiful intention and design. They reduce sex to an act and mistake your behavior for your identity, turning what you did into who you are. Cue the stats on the harmful effects of purity culture.

So, humans do what we do best: swing the pendulum all the way to the other side. We trade in shame for a free pass and tell people they can do whatever they want.

And that strategy works until it doesn't.
It's fun until it's not.

I have pastoral meetings all the time with people who are dealing with drama, shame, anger, or regret started by a situation that involved sex outside the boundaries God gave us. There's some irony here, isn't there? When we call Jesus's sexual ethic outdated, we're knocking the very worldview that would save us from so much pain. Despite the narrative of our day, the truth is, living with no boundaries is a recipe for betrayal, heartache, distrust, and chaos. It might be fun for a bit, but then it leaves us feeling even more isolated. Like we're trying to fix a deep wound with a few Band-Aids, all too aware that we'll always need just a few more.

Legalism leaves you with shame.
Recklessness leaves you with pain.

Welcome to the tension.

I won't pretend like I have the answer to the riddle. I don't know if there is one. Honestly, I think the truth about sexuality and singleness is less a problem to solve and more a tension to manage. That said, there are helpful (and unhelpful) ways to manage it.

Fortunately, Jesus gave us an example of how to handle it beautifully.

A Bunch of Stoners
A few chapters after Jesus talked to the woman at the well and then met with the man on the mat, he headed to the Feast of Tabernacles, one of three annual festivals when Jewish people from all over Israel made a pilgrimage to Jerusalem. This one was to remember God's provision during the forty years they wandered in the wilderness.

On the last day of the festival, Jesus stood and summed up part 1 of this book in two verses: "Let anyone who is thirsty come to me and drink. Whoever believes in me, as Scripture has said, rivers of living water will flow from within them."[9]

Remember, Jesus had a knack for stirring the water. He reminded the crowd that when we treat faith like just a list of things we have to do and festivals we have to attend, the water gets stagnant. But when we realize we can actually have a relationship with God, the water begins to stir—the stagnant water comes back to life.

Jesus dropped that truth bomb, and then everyone went back to their tents and went to bed.

But two people who weren't married to each other found themselves in the same tent. And got caught.

At dawn the next morning, Jesus headed right back into the temple courts and began teaching again. The religious leaders somehow caught the woman (interestingly enough, not the man) and brought her before Jesus.[10]

According to the law, this woman should've been stoned to death. Wherever the topic of sex and shame is discussed, there are bound to be some stoners hanging around, ready to hurl accusations and pronounce judgment. The stoners put Jesus in a corner to test him. Would he keep to the law and make the unpopular decision to end a life, or would he break the law?

It was a lose-lose.

The Pharisees wanted it that way. They wanted Jesus out. (When you're in charge, you have a vested interest in keeping the water stagnant.)

Tension was high. The religious leaders were on edge. The crowd was on edge. The woman was certainly on edge. Everyone was nervous except Jesus. He saw what no one else could. A hurt, broken, embarrassed woman who was terrified for her life. She'd made a mistake, and apparently, no one would let her forget it. But while everyone else was thinking about the principle, Jesus was looking at the person.

If you've heard the story, you know Jesus brilliantly invited anyone who had never made a mistake to go ahead and cast the first stone. But of course, none of them were able to do that. Most of the time, when we throw stones at others for their imperfections, it's because we're terrified to face our own. Jesus masterfully held up a mirror and snapped them out of their self-righteous stupor. One by one, they dropped their stones and walked away.

The stoners left with more self-awareness.
The woman left experiencing the grace and forgiveness of Jesus in a whole new way.

A Spoonful of Sugar

When I was a kid, I had a hard time swallowing medicine. My mom had a solution. I never had a problem eating pudding, so she would give me a spoonful of pudding with the pill hidden in it.

A play straight out of Mary Poppins's playbook: "A spoonful of sugar helps the medicine go down."[11] Which she actually got from Jesus:

> "Where are they? Has no one condemned you?"
> "No one, sir," she said.
> "Then neither do I condemn you," Jesus declared. "Go now and leave your life of sin."[12]

Tension was high, but Jesus stepped right into the middle of it with love. True love. The type of love that had two active ingredients: grace and truth. The pudding and the pill. The spoonful of sugar and the medicine.

Grace: I don't condemn you.
Truth: You don't have to keep falling into these same unhealthy patterns anymore.

Jesus is love in action.
This story is his master class.

If you dive a bit deeper into the story, you'll realize he took the same approach with the stoners:

Grace: Even though you spent the whole morning judging this woman, you can go free too.
Truth: If you're going to throw stones, be consistent. Hold yourself to the same standard you're holding her to.

The stoners got humbled, and the woman got liberated.

Jesus walked into a lose-lose.
And turned it into a win-win.

He lived in the tension where grace meets truth, each word drenched in both, and whenever people interacted with him, they gained the clarity and courage they needed to confront their past.

When you start approaching your past with both grace and truth, you'll find the same clarity and courage to confront your mistakes, call out the shame that keeps you stuck in yesterday, and start being present today.

That's what I needed to hear in the moments leading up to that sermon I was supposed to deliver. I was reluctant to go into the church because I was listening to the stoners instead of the Savior. I had traded in truth and grace for a half-truth with no grace. Doug was reminding me of this tension:

Grace: I can get up onstage and tell people about Jesus today.
Truth: I probably need to get some help tomorrow.

That's what I needed to hear. I hung up with Doug and walked into the church, worshipped, and then got up to preach, well aware of how unqualified I was. I wasn't trying to impress people or win them over; I was just up there, grateful to be an imperfect person who still gets to tell people about a perfect God.

To be honest, I don't remember what I said (neither does anyone else, by the way). But I'll never forget how I felt. I may have been down in the dirt, covered in shame, but I felt like Jesus was sitting right next to me the whole time. Reminding me that if this were about my good behavior, I would've been disqualified a long time ago.

It was a special night for me.

Truth: The standard for being in right standing with God is perfection.
Grace: Jesus is that perfection.

We all have a past. Understanding Jesus's approach is the starting point for confronting it. Yesterday will continue to beat you up until you realize your identity isn't determined by your behavior. When you confront your past in love (grace and truth), it begins to lose its hold on you.

Yesterday's shame slowly becomes today's triumph.

The proof, as they say, is in the pudding.

Do the Work
The morning after I preached, I woke up and decided I needed to change a few things about my life. I knew I was forgiven, but I would've been lying if I'd said Saturday night had no impact on Sunday—of course it did.

Grace: There is no condemnation for your sins.
Truth: There are consequences for them.

I decided it was time to get to work, so I signed up for a course designed to help me dig down under the surface and figure out why porn was my drug of choice. One of the most important questions the course taught me to ask was, *What am I medicating?*

There's a reason you keep going back to porn (or whatever your drug of choice is). At some level, you believe it's the solution to the pain you're feeling. The best way to become aware of that pain is to ask, *What am I medicating?*

I could fill an entire book with my answers, but I'll give you one, and then we'll talk about you. For me, a lot of my time and effort go toward trying to convince the world that I'm enough. As if my life is one big audition, everyone is a judge, and I'm trying to convince people that I have what it takes. I'm trying to land the role, to get the part.

I'm on a constant search for validation.

If I can say enough smart things for people to be drawn to me—I feel like I got the part that day.

If I can be witty enough to make people laugh—I feel like I got the part that day.

If I can wow people with a thought-provoking sermon—I feel like I got the part that day.

Unfortunately, validation from people is short-lived. Every time I go to bed, it resets. I wake up in the morning needing to prove myself all over again.

Getting the part is my greatest need.
Getting rejected is my greatest fear.

Whether or not you can relate, you can at least imagine how exhausting that is. When things are going well and the validation is flooding in, I feel pretty good. But when the validation stops, I start looking for it in other places. Enter porn.

Sex (in its purest form) is two people validating their love for each other. And although porn is obviously only a counterfeit version of that, in moments of weakness I get tricked into thinking it's the real thing. It medicates my pain for a moment. Dr. Mark Chamberlain, who has done a lot of work helping people sift through porn addiction, explained it like this: "To have another human being love us, want us, trust us, approve of us, just be delighted in us, that's wired into our systems to help us connect with other human beings." He went on to say that even though we may know the picture or video we're viewing is counterfeit, our brains don't realize it in the moment.[13]

It's all a façade that leaves me feeling way less worthy of love and validation by throwing me into a spiral of shame. The mature part of me knows not to seek validation from porn. But then urges, insecurities, and exhaustion sneak in, and I throw it all out, resonating all too well with these words from the apostle Paul: "I do not do the good I want to do, but the evil I do not want to do— this I keep on doing."[14]

I didn't experience any level of freedom until I started asking myself what I was medicating. A little bit of self-awareness goes a long way. Once I saw how much energy I was expending searching for validation, I got curious about why. For some people, the answer is obvious: a big-T traumatic event. For me, it's been a thousand little things. And I don't mean to oversimplify a complicated journey—there are way more layers to it—but when I start to feel pulled toward porn, it's helpful to remind myself that I'm searching for validation and that some image or video isn't the answer.

Grace: I'm searching for validation because I'm human.
Truth: God loves me, and that's all the validation I need.[15]

I don't mean to be the "next time just read the Bible" guy, but the truth is, it really does work.

What about you? What pain are you trying to medicate? Is it a search for validation? A search for significance? A search for connection? A search for peace?

Like so much of the rest of this book, my goal here is to help you get the conversation started. Learning to be content being single today is a process, and my goal is to help you take some initial steps down the path. Answering the question, *What am I medicating?* is a pivotal step. If that question is resonating with you at any level, follow it and see where it takes you. Bring some trusted people into the conversation, or even consider reaching out to a counselor or therapist.

Everyone has their own journey. But follow the path long enough, and you'll begin to realize a really important truth—intensity doesn't equal intimacy.

Intensity Isn't Intimacy

Our souls are searching for intimacy, but when we don't get what we're looking for, we start trying to find something else to fill that emptiness. When we can't find intimacy, we're prone to look for its counterfeit cousin. The cheap knockoff of intimacy—intensity.

Think about a one-night stand. God designed humans to meet, pursue, woo, fall in love, and then commit to each other emotionally, financially, geographically, and eventually physically. A one-night stand takes that entire sacred journey and presses it into one night. So, in the midst of it, your soul is fooled into believing it's experiencing the intimacy it's desperate for.

But it's a trick.
An illusion.

When you fall for it, you end up feeling duped and depleted. Empty, like your soul was being torn apart while it thought it was being put together. Then it feels the need to repeat the

process the next week—kind of like trying to quench your thirst
at the wrong well.

Porn is another example. An attempt to create an idealistic version of the beautiful gift of sex. It's a multi-billion-dollar industry
that spends its days creating more versions of this intensity to
confuse and trap people in their search for intimacy.

But it's a trick.
An illusion.

You end up feeling duped and depleted. Needing to repeat the
process the next week.

We're on an endless search for connection.
When we have it, we feel at peace, like our souls have come home.
When we lose it, we look for it.
When we can't find it, we settle for counterfeit versions.

It's no wonder porn is so addicting.

But the good news is, change is actually possible for you. Porn
has harmful effects on your brain, but research has shown that
those negative effects can be reversed.[16] As you stay away from it
for longer and longer, your brain can begin to reset and rediscover the true, intimate, God-given design for sex.

Part of doing the work is learning to discern between intensity
and intimacy. It's about taking time to breathe and ask why you
did what you did. So much of it happens beneath the surface, at a
subconscious level. The work is learning to see it. To call it out. To
shine a light on it.

Grace: God keeps no record of your wrongs.
Truth: Your mind does. And you'll keep going back to the same
old habits until you confront them.

Morning Light

I'm sure a run-in with a bunch of stoners wasn't how the woman in the story imagined her morning beginning. It was humiliating. Traumatizing. But then again, I bet an encounter with the Savior wasn't on her docket either.

As awful of a morning as that was, there must've been some magic in the moments that followed.

At some point, she looked around and realized she was still alive.
At some point, the adrenaline started to fade.
At some point, her mind began the uphill battle of trying to process the event.
At some point, her body let out the overwhelming quivers of fear she had locked up.

Absolutely.

But I wonder if there was a moment when she realized she was safe.

At some point, she became an afterthought to everyone except the Savior.
At some point, she must've glanced up and seen a new day, a new promise, a fresh start, dawning in the eastern sky.

The scene reminds me of Zechariah's prophecy about Jesus: "Because of God's tender mercy, the morning light from heaven is about to break upon us, to give light to those who sit in darkness and in the shadow of death, and to guide us to the path of peace."[17]

The morning light.

The promise that no matter how dark the night may be, grace comes in the morning. The reminder that where there is light, there cannot be darkness.

Maybe it's time for you to discover (or rediscover) that today is a new day. God loves you today, just the way you are. He is also giving you an invitation to leave all the old, unhelpful patterns behind. To experience the true freedom that comes with practicing living like Jesus.

Truth: You won't get it right all the time.
Grace: That's the point.

Marriage isn't a prerequisite for abundant life; it can't be. I know this because Jesus wasn't married. That abundant life is possible for you—it really is. You just need to step into the beautiful, mysterious tension between grace and truth.

Grace: God loves you right where you are.
Truth: God loves you too much to let you stay there.

Disagree with the grace part, and you'll remain a prisoner to the shame of the past.

Disagree with the truth part, and you'll repeat the past.

But embrace the grace and the truth and you can start to experience freedom.

Transformation is possible. If the Bible teaches us anything, it's that tomorrow doesn't have to be like today.

Do the work. Keep asking yourself what you're medicating. Keep going through the ups and downs. Keep fighting. Keep confessing. Keep getting help. Stay curious about why you're doing what you're doing. Stir the water, because the stagnant water in your soul is meant to be a river of living water.

Once you begin stirring the stagnant water from yesterday, you'll notice yourself being more present today. But before we move on, there is one final piece to releasing the past. It's one thing to stir the water every once in a while, but it's better to create a system that keeps the water moving constantly.

To explain what I mean, we have to talk about the happiest place on earth.

Chapter 4

The Happiest Place on Earth

Set Up a System That Stirs

Time keeps moving forward. Have you noticed?

Part 1 of this book has been all about letting go of yesterday. The tricky part is that, by tomorrow, today will be another yesterday. There will always be more past to let go of.

In the first three chapters, we've done a lot of work to let go of moments from the past, but the truth is that this has to be an ongoing practice. The trick isn't just to stir the water; it's to set up a system where the water is always stirring. And for that, we need to take a trip to the happiest place on earth.

On July 17, 1955, Walt Disney's dream became a reality.[1]

He opened Disneyland on 160 acres in Anaheim, California, bringing the magic of stories and animations to life. Less than a decade later, Walt, forever the optimist and innovator, set his mind on something a little bigger.[2] Not just a theme park but an entire world—Disney World.

That would require a lot more land, so he looked east and found 27,400 acres in the middle of Florida that he could buy for a fraction of the price he'd paid in California.[3]

Walt was convinced he could transform the land into the happiest place on earth. But there was one problem. The land was in the

middle of a giant swamp, in the middle of a state that is 31 percent wetland.[4] Florida has a lot of great qualities, but its abun-
dance of stagnant water isn't one of them. Swamps are gross and
uninviting, and worst of all, they're the place mosquitoes lay their
eggs.

When I get to heaven, I'll have a lot of questions for God. Questions I've spent my whole life thinking about, like God's sover-
eignty and our free will. "I've spent decades answering questions
about it," I'll tell him. "Was I anywhere close to being right?"

I imagine he'll say, "No, but you meant well."

But here's the big one, the ace up my sleeve. "God, why mosquitoes? All they do is cause problems." Which is true. Hundreds of
thousands of people die from mosquito bites every year, making
them the most dangerous animal alive.[5] Mosquitoes are annoying
at best and deadly at worst. "What's the deal, God?"

I'd imagine Walt Disney was asking the same question. Happiness
and mosquito bites are like oil and water; no matter how hard
you try, they just don't mix—so the happiest place on earth can't
be swarming with mosquitoes.

Enter the unsung hero of Disney World: Joe Potter.

Walt and Joe had become good friends. He was a retired army
general who specialized in designing systems. I picture him like
one of those guys who sees life like a giant game of Tetris, who
can pack an entire house worth of furniture into a tiny U-Haul.

Walt told his friend about the predicament, and he got to work.
In 2021, Christopher Lucas did an interview with the *Tampa Bay
Times,* and he said this about Joe: "He insisted to Walt, whatever
we do, wherever there's water, we got to make sure it's either running off, moving or it's just not sitting there or you're going to

have a lot of mosquitoes."[6] If stagnant water was the problem, that meant they had to design a park that kept every drop of water moving. Alongside his team, Joe thought through every square inch of Disney World.[7]

Water rides were set up to keep the water constantly recycled. Pools were given fountains in the middle, pushing the water out. Buildings were constructed to keep rainwater running down. Even the leaves on fake trees were designed to make sure they don't catch any water.[8]

If you ever make it down to Disney World, you'll notice two things. The first is there is no stagnant water. The second is you'll hardly ever see a mosquito.

The happiest place on earth can't have mosquitoes. So Disney World went (and continues to go) to great lengths to give people a vacation from those flying, bloodsucking beasts.

I say all that to say this: *Walt and Joe got it.* They understood a concept at an architectural level that we, as single people, need to learn at a soul level.

Stirring the water is helpful only if you also fix the structure that allowed the water to get stagnant in the first place. We all have a leaf we could reshape or a rafter we could alter to keep things moving.

One day, during a session of spiritual direction, I started wondering why I settle for stagnation when I was born to have rivers of living water flowing from within. I decided it was time to summon my inner Joe Potter and think through every square inch of my life. Every word I say, every reaction I have, and every unhealthy pattern I fall into.

I told Bill about the endeavor and asked him if he had any recommendations for where to start. I figured, after all those sessions, he'd have noticed some blind spots to point out, and I was sure he'd have a nice long list. But giving me a few items to work on is the type of answer a novice gives; Bill is an expert.

"You already know where to start," he said.

"No, I don't," I shot back. "That's why I asked."

"Yes, you do," he said calmly. "You just need to learn to listen to yourself."

I drove home, shaking my head, wondering why I still paid Bill for sessions of vague advice. But a few weeks later, I had a conversation in Laguna Beach that brought a lot of clarity.

I Don't Care. . . . I Don't Care

During those days, when I was learning how to go to counseling more and sit stuck in church parking lots less, Laguna Beach was my home away from home. It was only a twenty-five-minute drive, and my good friend Sam had an apartment a block from the beach. We both took Mondays off, and since he was also a single pastor, "off" meant truly off.

Our other pastor friends were starting to get married, have kids, and spend their Mondays changing diapers. Not us. We spent our Mondays on the beach. Surfing, reading, sleeping, and repeating.

Every Monday.
For years.
It was glorious.

Sam was the youth pastor at a local church that met on Tuesday nights. Every once in a while, I would drive down there and speak.

On one particular night, Sam's mom, Sally, was there. Sally is a legend in Laguna, a famous painter, but we all know her for her ability and passion to mentor the next generation.

I ran into Sally in the lobby before service, and we started catching up. Our conversation was cut short as cars arrived at the church—high schoolers jumping out of vehicles as the parents gave that confused, "What is this thing I'm dropping my kids at again?" look and then sped off.

Sally and I were wrapping up our conversation and getting ready to make this night about the kids when a freshman girl ran up and barged into our conversation.

"My boyfriend just broke up with me, but I don't care."

As a guy who hates small talk, I think that's a fantastic way to start a conversation.

"I don't care," she said smugly. "He said he wanted to see other people, but I don't care." And then she walked off.

"Hmmm," Sally said, smiling at the idea of the two of us being thrown into the middle of Laguna Beach High School's drama. She's a sage—a master of the craft—who knows what's going on in people's souls before they do. "I don't care. I don't care," she said with a smile. "I think that means she cares."

I started laughing. Sally, being the better person, walked after her to continue the conversation.

That moment stayed with me. Sally's words gave legs to Bill's advice. When I don't know what needs to change about my life, the answer is usually right under my nose. It's the thing I'm busy trying to convince myself I don't care about.

Want to confront your past but don't know where to begin? Start with the thing you try the hardest to pretend you don't care about. That's probably the thing you care about the most.

Here's an example: You love being single; you're always telling your friends how much you enjoy it. However, the truth is, every few weeks a deep darkness sets in late at night, and you begin feeling lonely and start asking existential questions about being perpetually alone. But when the thoughts pop up, you push them down and tell yourself you don't care.

I don't care.
I don't care.
I think that means you care.

Or you start to notice a problematic pattern in your dating life. Every time you meet someone you like, you panic and push them away, immediately lose interest, or get way too invested way too fast and scare them away. But whenever you see the pattern and wonder if you'll be able to overcome the obstacle, you force the thought away.

I don't care.
I don't care.
I think that means you care.

Or what about that feeling you get deep down in your gut when all your friends start getting married?

I don't care.
I don't care.
I think that means you care.

Do you resonate with that one? I certainly do. Instead of pretending, let's face the pain head on and talk about that feeling we get when all our friends start becoming permanent couples.

Permanent Couples

Fires are magical. Mesmerizing. Full of amazing potential to warm and awful potential to destroy.

Some of my favorite nights have taken place around bonfires. Sunsets on the beach, cooking fish over an open fire. Cold nights in the Rocky Mountains, where Bible verses like "Count the stars, if you are able" push you to your limit as you huddle around the flames, eating s'mores.[9] Or a simple firepit in a friend's backyard, where the view may not be as good but the conversation makes up for it.

Around the time my brother talked me out of walking away from ministry, I had one of those memorable nights around a fire with friends.

Some good friends of mine got engaged and threw a party to celebrate. They didn't hold back—food, toasts, games, and a ton of laughter. Once everyone else filed out, we ended the night around a bonfire. Because, at every party, there's the crowd, and then there's the community—the people who stick around to clean up and often end up around a fire.

Toward the end of the night, I glanced at my phone and saw I'd missed a barrage of texts—all in a group thread from the guys I went on that yearlong trip with. The first was a screen capture of an Instagram post. The second simply said, "The one that got away."

Let's back up for a minute. Do you remember how I told Bill in our first session that I wasn't interested in dating? That was something I call "a mostly complete truth"—a statement that is completely true, most of the time. Because I wasn't interested, most of the time. However, a year prior, I was kind of interested in someone for a bit and even went on three dates. But then, in the same old pattern, I realized I wasn't invested enough to commit to anything and called it off. Three dates may not feel like much to you, but for a guy who has been on only a handful of dates his whole life, three was a lot.

My friends weren't the only ones celebrating their engagement that night. The Instagram post was that girl with her now fiancé; a long string of roasts and fantastic jokes from my three friends followed.

Everyone could tell that I'd completely disengaged from the conversation around the fire. "The last person I ever dated just got engaged," I told them, trying to justify my absence.

"How do you feel about that?" one of my more perceptive friends asked.

"I mean, I don't really care," I said nonchalantly. "I'm happy for her. I don't care."

Uh-oh . . .

I don't care.
I don't care.
I think that means I care.

The words felt insincere as soon as they came out of my mouth. I thought of Bill sitting in his chair, eyebrows raised in invitation (not condemnation).

Others began sharing their own stories of similar situations, tapping into their feelings and talking about how weird it was. "Well, actually," I said to the group, their words giving me the courage to say what everyone already knew. "It feels . . . It feels . . ." I stammered, cursing myself for leaving Keith's list of emotions at home. "Strange."

I'm not sure what I think is going to happen when I practice being vulnerable with people I love. I'm not sure why there is a voice somewhere telling me it's a bad idea. But I shared my honest thoughts, and nothing bad happened. Nothing bad ever really happens. Everyone just nodded and continued launching into their own tales of times that heartbreak happened to them.

Singleness changes when the people around you start getting married. In high school and college, most of your friends are single. Besides Cory and Topanga, who always had it together,* all your friends are in the same boat as you. They may date someone for the summer, but for the most part, relationships don't last.

Somewhere along the way, that starts to change—summer flings turn into wedding rings.

It's easier to be lackadaisical about singleness before people start staking claims. Once proposals, bachelor/bachelorette parties, and weddings start happening, the stakes rise really quick. You get a lot of moments to realize all your friends are moving forward with their lives romantically, and you begin wondering if that means you're falling behind.

In chapter 2, we talked about the ones that got away. Whenever the ones that got away get engaged, it's an odd feeling.

A missed opportunity turns into *a lost opportunity.*
Maybe one day becomes *not ever any day.*

And if we're being honest, it's strange. I bet you know the feeling.

"Yeah, I saw pictures of their wedding, but I don't care. I'm happy for them; I don't care about our past."

---

*   If you don't know, that's a *Boy Meets World* reference.

I don't care.
I don't care.
I think that means you care.

Of course you care.
Of course that hurts.
Of course it's weird.

At one point, you were wondering if you wanted to marry them, and now they're building out that dream with someone else. It could've been you, and it's not. Weird.

Pretending that isn't strange isn't helpful.
But then again, neither is jealousy.

Talking to my friends that night around the fire, I realized my jealousy was me trying to freeze the past—trying to hold on to yesterday. To keep things the way they were. But that's not how life works. There's the way I wanted things to go, and then there's the way they went. Two different outcomes.

Jealousy creates division in your soul. Jealousy tries to hold on to the past while, in reality, life is busy moving forward.

That's confusing.
And confusion leads to frustration.
And frustration leads to apathy.
And apathy leads to stagnation.
And stagnation is fertile ground for mosquito eggs.

Jealousy is like a spa for mosquitoes. Those bloodsuckers love that stagnant water. Like a bunch of high schoolers missing the point of a coffee shop, they'll hang out all day without giving you a dime. And your soul can't be the happiest place on earth with winged vampires hatching everywhere.

Do you resonate with that? If you do, don't feel bad. Jealousy is a problem for every human; it has a subtle way of taking down the best of us. It feels good in the moment, but it doesn't lead to life.

James, Jesus's own brother, understood the danger of jealousy. I'd imagine he had plenty of moments when he felt like he was living in his brother's shadow; maybe sometimes jealousy would start to creep in. By the time he wrote his letter, he knew the truth. He knew there's no good fruit of jealousy. He wrote, "Wherever there is jealousy and selfish ambition, there you will find disorder and evil of every kind."[10]

That jealousy you're holding on to isn't serving you; it's only creating disorder in your life. By pulling you back to some event that happened in the past, it's keeping you from being present today.

So, what do you do? What do you do if you don't want to let jealousy rule your life? How can you create a system that keeps the water stirring so much that envy and bitterness have no chance to grow in your life?

The answer is gratitude. You have to set up a system that keeps you thankful for what you do have today instead of thinking about what you missed out on yesterday.

Gratitude and Today

Walt Disney was one of the most creative minds of the twentieth century. Isn't it interesting that one of our best thinkers dedicated his life to creating happiness? To giving people a place where they can escape their own reality and get lost in a fantasy world.

And at some level, it works—which is why we'll spend $150 to get in.
And $50 to eat lunch.
And $5 for a churro.
And $35 for Mickey ears.

And then another $5 for another churro.
All because we want to be happy.
And it works, kind of.

But some of the happiest people on earth have never been to Disney World.
And other people throw a fit if the line is too long for It's a Small World.

The trick, I've come to believe, has less to do with your circumstances and more to do with how you design your inner world. It has less to do with everything going right and more to do with putting your architect hat on (do architects wear hats?) and fixing the places in your soul where the water stagnates.

I don't care.
I don't care.
I think that means you care.

So instead of ignoring that person, thing, or event, or making another joke about it, dive into the deep water and stir it up by practicing gratitude today. Few things work as rapidly to stir the water in your soul as being thankful for what you have. I don't just mean the cheap, knockoff version of gratitude where we say thanks for things in an obligatory way, like the text messages friends send each other on Thanksgiving. That's a good exercise, but it's pretty powerless when you're up against your ex's wedding reel.

I mean the type of gratitude that's more of a decision than a feeling. A decision to look for the good in the situation and focus on the things you have today instead of the ones you miss from yesterday.

The type of gratitude that reminds you that you still have breath in your lungs.

The type of gratitude that watches a sunset and marvels at the beauty of the colors instead of complaining that you have no one to watch it with.

The type of gratitude that appreciates a great bite of food or the perfect cup of coffee instead of focusing on the empty seat across from you.

The type of gratitude that reminds you how beautiful it is to be alive—regardless of your relationship status.

Jealousy complains about what is missing. Gratitude rejoices in what is present.

Singleness is a gift. It really is. But if you are single and don't want to be, you probably don't see it that way. Gratitude is the decision to be single today. To play the hand you've been dealt to the best of your ability.

Jealousy likes to pull you back to yesterday, but gratitude grounds you in today. It's hard to stay bitter about the past when you're happy about where you are. If you want your own soul to be the happiest place on earth, you have to design gratitude into your day.

At least, that's the thought I had as I sat around the fire. I could let that Instagram post throw me down a spiral of jealousy that would lead to bitterness. Or I could look up and notice the amazing friends surrounding me. The people in my life today.

That doesn't mean that seeing your ex's honeymoon photos isn't strange; it just means you're going to make the conscious decision to embrace where you are. You may not be with that person anymore, but look at the people you have in your life. You're probably doing better than you think and probably have more to be thankful for than you realize. You just have to embrace the present with gratitude and decide to be single today.

As an aside, if their posts do throw you for a loop, unfollowing someone takes about five seconds—that's time well spent. I'll gladly be the one to give you permission to hit unfollow. You're not being mean to them; you're being nice to yourself. Don't overthink it; go for it.

A System That Stirs

If you've been doing the work, you've probably noticed two things. The first is that change is actually possible; the second is that it takes a lot of effort. You can talk a big game about your goal to release the past and be single today, but if you really want to change, you have to build practices into your day to keep it happening.

James Clear, author of the bestselling book *Atomic Habits,* said it well: "You do not rise to the level of your goals. You fall to the level of your systems."[11] Setting the goal to be content being single today is great, but setting up a system that keeps you grateful for your life and grounded in this present moment is the secret. You need a system that stirs.

My friend Adam and I learned this lesson the hard way during the pandemic in 2020. Adam was about to get married but needed a place to live until his wedding, so he moved into my spare bedroom for a few months. Remember that summer? I'm thankful he was there, because it was a strange time.

We all have our own stories and struggles from those days. I had to be part of figuring out how to move church online. I went from preaching to people to talking to a camera. And from meeting with actual people in real life to Zoom calls.

It wasn't the same, and I couldn't help but miss the days before the pandemic—I started giving way more mental attention to yesterday than to today. And I could feel my soul getting stagnant.

One night, Adam and I decided we needed to change things up. We needed to set up a system for our mornings that would ground us in today and help us be present.

The system we decided on was simple but effective. We'd work out in the garage every morning from 7:00 to 7:40, then sit in the backyard from 7:40 to 8:00 and share three things we were grateful for.

That's it.

It may sound like a small thing, but it made a big change. A simple system has the power to make a big impact. As the Tanzanian proverb reminds us, "Little by little, a little becomes a lot." Because when you know you have another gratitude check-in coming, you start to keep your eyes open all day for things to add to your gratitude list. You spend less time missing the past, and more time enjoying the present.

In a summer where the world grew stagnant, we set up a system that stirred.

Do you have a system for your singleness? A system that keeps you from getting stuck in the past? Here's a simple plan:

Morning: Start the day with a list of three things you're thankful for. Find a friend who wants to join you on this journey, and commit to texting each other three things you're thankful for every morning before 10:00.

Afternoon: Set an alarm on your phone for every afternoon at 3:00. When it goes off, stop for three minutes and pick one thing you're thankful for and one person you're praying for. Thank God for whatever that thing is, and then say a prayer for the neighbor, friend, co-worker, or family member you're thinking about.

Evening: Before you watch a show or unwind for the night, grab your journal and spend five minutes processing your day. What is one good thing that happened today? How did it make you feel, and why are you so grateful? Obviously, feel free to write out the tough parts of your day, too, but make sure you either begin or end with gratitude.

That's a simple system, but it will keep the water in your soul stirring. With consistency, you'll notice it getting easier to let go of yesterday and stay focused on today.

You aren't going to get it perfect, but perfection isn't the point. The point is to be present right where you are. After all, this is the only moment we can truly be with God.

My past is messy. So is yours. You can heal parts of it. You can forgive. You can repent. You can go to therapy. And you should. But then at some point, you need to take a breath and choose to be grateful for where you are today. The truth is, you're probably doing better than you think.

Do the work, but don't obsess over it.
Confront your past, and then be content with where you are.
Set up a system, and then trust the process.
Be proud of how far you've come, and then laugh about how far you still have to go.
Be honest about yesterday, and then release it and practice being single today.

But before we get to today in part 3, we have some more work to do. First we're going to learn about Mary of Bethany's first interaction with Jesus, what it may've taught her about her past, and what it can teach us about ours. Then it'll be time to move on to part 2. Yesterday is only the first enemy of singleness. There's another enemy crouching in the corner, content to let you duke it out with yesterday before moving in for the kill: tomorrow.

If we want to be single today, we have to talk about our propensity to obsess about the future.

Well, part 1 was good and all, but I don't think I need part 2. I don't care about tomorrow. Sure, the future wakes me up in a pool of sweat and keeps me up at night, but I don't care.

Uh-oh.

I don't care.
I don't care.
Everyone together now: I think that means you care!

Stir the Stagnant Water

Her sister was stressed. She'd later say she wasn't, but Mary knew her well. She shook her head as Martha raced through the kitchen, scrubbing the same spot she'd already cleaned three times.

Mary always respected her sister's passion for hosting people, even though she never felt the same. She struggled to feel much of anything these days.

It hadn't always been that way. There was a time when she felt alive, a time when having visitors would excite her, when she'd be the life of the party, the one making jokes and telling stories late into the night. That felt like an eternity ago. These days, she longed for any social event to end so she could go to bed.

Numb was her preferred state. Opting to stay closed off and distant from everyone except her sister. What Martha called a boring lifestyle Mary called wisdom. Life was too painful, and it was too risky to trust anyone.

At least, that's what she kept telling herself.
Day after day.
Week after week.
Month after month.

Hoping the narrative that people couldn't be trusted would distract her from her soul's stagnant state.

There was a knock on the door. The Rabbi and his followers were there, all smiles. The crew came through the door with greetings and laughter, tossing full wineskins down on the table and thanking Mary and Martha for hosting.

Mary took a deep breath, hyping herself up in an attempt to be present. Her sister, meanwhile, never seemed to struggle with that. She was in game mode, racing around the room, bringing out food, and hosting the evening with passion.

The night was lively at first. There was never any shortage of conversation with this crew, but slowly, naturally, the tone became more subdued, and everyone's attention shifted to Jesus, who began speaking in a way Mary had never heard.

"Anyone who wants to be first must be the very last."
"Whoever wants to become great among you must be your servant."
"Whoever finds their life will lose it, and whoever loses their life for my sake will find it."

Mary had heard her fair share of teaching, but this was different. Seemingly backward or upside down and yet, in some mysterious way, right side up. As if Jesus was talking about the way things were always supposed to be. Something stirred deep within her. Something in her soul. She held on to every word as the group moved to the back room. The disciples smiled as if remembering the first time they heard these teachings. They nodded to Mary, a silent invitation for her to join them.

As her sister rushed through the room, refilling drinks and offering more food, Mary sat, listening and responding to each word. She couldn't remember the last time she'd been this interested in a conversation.

"What do you think, Martha?"
Mary could tell the Rabbi's question caught her sister off guard.

"I, uh," she started. "I . . . I . . . am going to run next door and
grab another wineskin from the neighbor. I'll be right back."

Mary gave her sister a look, a look they'd shared many times before, but Martha wasn't having it. "Jesus, tell Mary to come help
me."

"Martha," Jesus answered, "you are worried and upset about
many things, but few things are needed—or indeed only one. Mary
has chosen what is better, and it will not be taken away from her."

He looked knowingly at Mary, who sat at his feet, listening to
what he had to say, and smiled. Mary's heart started racing. She
knew what he had just given them: a call that ran much deeper
than just an invitation to slow down and hang out. Jesus was offering her and her sister the invitation every good Israelite longed
to hear from a rabbi.

Follow me.
Sit at my feet.
Learn the way.
Then go and do likewise.

Jesus was inviting Mary and Martha into a life of purpose and
meaning, and the invitation was shattering a dam deep in Mary's
soul, sweeping away years of pain and pessimism.

Emotions flooded back into her body. Jubilation, gratitude, embarrassment, uncertainty, even fear and pain. She welcomed each
one—all preferred over feeling nothing at all. The disciples were
smiling; their reassuring looks eased the discomfort, as if they had
similar stories. She took a deep breath—her first in many moons.

She could feel.
She could smile.
She could laugh.

The water in her soul was stirring.

Mary and You

There's a lot we can learn from the three interactions Mary of Bethany had with Jesus. This first story is somewhat famous. Mary and Martha hosted Jesus and his disciples, and while Martha spent the evening running around and trying to be a good host, Mary sat at Jesus's feet. Remember, Jesus was a rabbi. Sitting at the feet of a rabbi was the posture of a disciple, someone who was ready to learn.

We don't know what Jesus said to Mary that night, but he once told Peter and Andrew to leave their past as fishermen and step into purpose today. He once told Matthew to turn from tax collecting and follow him today. I'm speculating a bit, but there's a good chance he was helping Mary let go of her past and see the invitation to be a part of the movement. To let go of yesterday and step into her purpose today.

The same invitation is on the table for you. When we're single, it can be difficult to believe that Jesus is calling us to step up and be a part of what he is doing, but he is. Marriage has never been a prerequisite for ministry.

But if you're going to be a part of what Jesus is doing today, he'll call you to let go of some things from yesterday. The goal of part 1 of this book has been to help you do that. Before you move on to part 2, take some time to reflect on everything you read by answering the following questions.

For Reflection and Discussion

1. Did part 1 of this book bring up any memories that you haven't thought about in a long time? What emotions do you associate with each memory? Regret? Fear? Shame? Anger? Take a few minutes to give them a name and give them some space by writing about them in a journal.

2. As you read part 1, was there anything you felt that God was inviting you to leave in your past so you can step into what he has for you today?

3. Do you have someone in your life who helps you stir the water? Someone who asks you questions about your past, gives you room to process, and genuinely cares about you? If so, reach out and thank them. If not, what is one step you can take this week to find someone? (Have an honest conversation with a trusted friend or family member, or seek out a paid professional.)

4. As you read the first few chapters of this book, was there another single person on your mind who would benefit from joining you in reading this? Going through this journey with someone will make it way more beneficial. Consider reaching out to them and inviting them along for the ride.

PART TWO

Tomorrow

Do not worry about tomorrow,
for tomorrow will worry about itself.
—Matthew 6:34

PART 1 WAS ABOUT STIRRING the stagnant water in your soul, because when you don't have a Jeff or Judy to keep the water moving, you have to be more intentional about finding ways to keep the past from paralyzing you. But if stirring the stagnant water was all it took for us to thrive while being single today, this book would be a lot shorter.

There's a second enemy of singleness: tomorrow.

If stirring the stagnant water is the solution for the soul stuck in the past, then stilling the rough water is the solution for the soul worried about the future.

Rough water is murky, unpredictable, and dangerous. You can't rest in it. No one takes their inner tube out on class five rapids to unplug for an afternoon. There's too much energy flowing through rough water to find peace in the present moment.

A soul consumed by tomorrow will always have difficulty navigating today confidently, so in part 2, we're going to learn how to still the rough water.

One quick note before we get into it. There's a big difference between *still* and *stagnant* water. The difference can be defined with a single word: *intention*.

Think about rest. When you finally have a day off after an intense stretch of work, you can make that rest intentional by asking yourself what would bring you life today: a hike, hanging out with friends, or a movie marathon by yourself. Going into it with the intention to rest will bear good fruit. Or you can opt out of checking in with yourself and just zone out on the couch all day, mindlessly flipping through Netflix with one hand while you scroll through social media with the other.

The first option leads to rest and clarity—still water.
The second option leads to restlessness and cloudiness—stagnant water.

Part 2 is about intentionally stilling the anxious water in your soul. It's about taking a deep breath and surrendering your fear of the future. Learning to still the rough water is like strengthening a muscle. It may be weak at the moment, but the more you exercise it, the stronger it gets, and the easier it becomes to walk around with a calm soul. You'll worry less, understand more, see more clearly—and before you know it, you'll start laughing about tomorrow while you continue enjoying today.

Chapter 5

The Tomorrow Trap

Develop a Plan for the Panic

These were the questions raging in my head as soon as I woke up this morning:

> *Am I going to be single for the rest of my life?*
> *I say I want to be, but do I really mean it?*
> *Will I regret this when I'm older?*
> *Why am I writing this book? Will that make it permanent? What if I change my mind?*
> *Wait. Why does my back hurt?*
> *I've been sleeping for the last eight hours. Who gets hurt sleeping?*
> *Am I getting old?*
> *Is my window of opportunity for meeting someone closing?*
> *Is there something wrong with me?*

Some version of those thoughts pops up in my mind most days—they're on my greatest-hits album. I'll be out enjoying a great meal with good friends, but then I'll get in my car and drive home, and the thoughts will strike out of nowhere.

I call it the tomorrow trap. And I fall into it all the time.

The tomorrow trap makes me worry about what singleness means for my future: *Are all my friends heading in a different direction?*

The tomorrow trap keeps me anxious about tomorrow: *Is it only going to get harder to meet someone if I decide I want to?*

The tomorrow trap leaves me stuck playing out hypotheticals: *What about kids? If I have them, they'll be much younger than my friends' kids.*

Trap is the right word, isn't it? No one plans their day around getting stuck in those thoughts. The tomorrow trap catches us by surprise, like a bear trap closing on a poor, unsuspecting fawn.

The tomorrow trap is a problem for everyone (regardless of relationship status), but the intensity is cranked up when you're single. The trap is often triggered by good questions from well-meaning people.

Here's one of the biggest questions for me: "Do you have the gift of singleness?" I get asked that all the time. Today I love it. But back then, it would often throw me for a loop. One moment always sticks out to me more than the others.

The Gift of Singleness

"Can I ask you a question?" The questioner was a friend, someone I trust. Her voice was shaking like whatever she was about to ask was something that had bothered her for too long.

More than a year had passed since I started going to spiritual direction with Bill, and I barely recognized the version of myself that was stuck in the church parking lot that fateful Sunday night. I'd done a lot of work to confront my past, and I felt free. But the other side of the coin still terrified me: the future.

It was another Sunday night, and we were locking up the church for the week. But I couldn't make it out the door without fielding one more question: "Do you think you have the gift of singleness?"

In the last ten years, I've gotten that question about ten thousand times. Probably, in part, because I'm a pastor. You may not get that exact question all the time, but I'm betting you get questions that are asking the same thing at the core.

Paul talked about gifts in his letters in the Bible. He said the Spirit gives us gifts like administration, craftsmanship, or prophecy— things that come naturally. And then, in 1 Corinthians 7, he started talking about his singleness, said it's actually the better option, and wrote, "I wish that all of you were as I am [single]. But each of you has your own gift from God; one has this gift, another has that."[1]

So, when you see lists of spiritual gifts, singleness will often be on there.

Now, listing singleness as a gift has brought up a lot of sharp debate over the years—and has caused a lot of pain. The debate is about whether Paul was calling singleness the gift or whether he was calling celibacy the gift. The pain is caused when a person who has had a genuine desire for a spouse for years but is still single is told it's because they have the gift of singleness.

Can you see why that would be confusing? It makes the single person feel like God has given them a desire and is withholding their desire from them at the same time. If that's been your experience, I'm sorry. While it's true that God's timeline may be a lot slower than you wish it was, it's not helpful to frame it in a way that makes it feel like you were dealt an unlucky hand—your friend got something cool like wisdom and you got stuck with singleness.

The core issue here, I believe, has nothing to do with today, and everything to do with tomorrow. If you are single but want to be married, you're well aware that you're single today. It's not breaking news. Your fear is that you're going to be single the rest of your life, and often when we call it "the gift of singleness," we make it sound like a life sentence.

I know this because of the sheer quantity of times I've been asked, and that brings us back to that Sunday evening at church.

"What do you mean?" I asked my friend, knowing full well where the conversation was heading.

"Well, because, you know, like Paul from the Bible . . . Are you living that Paul life?"

"Paul life?" I said, playing dumb. "What's that?"

That went on for a few minutes, and then she eventually asked the question she really wanted to ask: "Are you going to be single for the rest of your life?"

That's the question beneath the question.
That's what people actually want to know.

You can see why that question would be offensive to the person who has been genuinely seeking a spouse for years but is still single. Because we're always thinking about the future, especially when it comes to relationships.

When you're single, people put this weird pressure on you to date. But then go on a few dates, and they want you to get engaged. Once you propose, you get an hour of celebrating before people ask if you've set a date for the wedding, and after the wedding, you barely get the honeymoon before everyone starts wondering about kids.

It's like we're consumed with the next step, tormented by tomorrow. Like there's an hourglass timer on the shelf, each grain of sand mocking us as it falls. The hardest part about being single today is the way culture tells us to worry about tomorrow.

I didn't have language for that at the time, so instead, I just gave her an awkward non-answer and then spent my entire Monday overthinking it.

When people ask us about the gift of singleness, they're usually just curious. They don't realize that the question baits us right into the tomorrow trap. Do you ever feel the panic of being pulled out of today by being asked about tomorrow? Or the worry that sets in when you think you might be single forever? Or the stress of wondering if your loneliness is only going to get worse? The tomorrow trap can be vicious.

Over the years, I've learned it's helpful to have a plan for when the panic sets in. Unfortunately, I learned that lesson the hard way—at a wedding of all places.

Today Is My Teacher

"All right, party people, let's get all the married couples on the dance floor!" Wedding DJs have notoriously cheesy voices; this guy's had an extra level of cringe. (Admittedly, my insecurity has probably altered this memory a bit, giving him an exaggerated dose of inauthenticity. But it never feels good to be the only one not allowed on the dance floor, especially when you were the one officiating the wedding.)

The weekend after my friend asked me if I had the gift of single-ness, I officiated a wedding. By that point, I'd been performing weddings for about two years and hadn't managed to screw up any too badly. I really enjoyed them. Plus, there's usually alcohol involved, which means the audience is a bit quicker to laugh and is in a notably better mood than those on Sunday mornings.

The problem is the reception. Especially when you're an introverted pastor who doesn't know anyone at the wedding besides the bride and groom (who always seem to be a little too busy at their own reception to make small talk with me).

Back in those days, I thought it was my job to stick it out, to stay and meet people and dance. Until one of my pastor friends changed my life by pointing out that they probably didn't want me there either. *Huh, I never thought about that.*

On this particular evening, every person attending the wedding was married. I know that because I was the only one sitting during the anniversary dance.

"If you've been married longer than a year," the cheesy DJ continued, "remain on the dance floor." Besides the bride and groom, who were only an hour and a half in, no one left. They all kept dancing. Meanwhile, I sat alone at table 13, contemplating eating everyone's dessert.

"Okay, if you've been married five years or longer, remain on the dance floor." A few couples laughed and made their way back to their tables. But not to mine. I was holding down the fort. The walls felt like they were closing in on me. My face felt flushed; my lungs felt constricted. The anniversary dance is meant to celebrate the couple that's been married the longest. Instead, it had the opposite effect. It highlighted the single officiant sitting alone at table 13, wondering what he was doing at this reception.

The tomorrow trap saw its opportunity and seized it like a skilled predator stalking its prey.

Everyone's looking at me.
I'm ruining this moment.
Look how long they've all been married. I'm not even trying to meet someone.

My lifestyle is going to disqualify me from ever being part of the
final couple dancing.
Is there something wrong with me?

I was trying to breathe but couldn't. The tomorrow trap had me
in a half nelson, forcing me to tap out.

Certain moments highlight singleness. Weddings are big ones,
and so are holidays. In the next chapter, we'll talk about showing
up to weddings on your own, because there's an art to it—we'll
get there.

But back to the single officiant, sitting at a table by himself, having a mild panic attack during the anniversary dance. I'd sat
through anniversary dances before, but never as the lone ranger.
"If you've been married ten years or longer, stay on the dance
floor." The reception hall finally felt more balanced, but apparently, they'd stuck me at the advanced table (probably because
they didn't really think I would stay). All my tablemates were still
going strong.

"And now, if you've been married twenty-five years or longer,
keep dancing." That was the magic number. I was glad to regain
my tablemates, doing my best to blend back in with the group.
Their company helped. They smiled. I smiled back and found my
breath again.

The rough water started to calm down—to still. As it did, I had to
laugh at myself. In the words of Ron Burgundy, "That escalated
quickly."

During every big or sentimental event, the tomorrow trap is waiting nearby, ready to convince you that your current circumstance
is a forever thing. It's a disrupter, stealing you right out of the
present moment and making you feel like you're stuck, doomed
to remain where you are the rest of your days.

Ever felt that? Ever fallen into the hunter's crafty snare? It happens to the best of us. But when you're single, the snare has an extra sting.

When you fall in, you have two options. The first is to sit in the trap and throw yourself a pity party (my preferred method). The second is to ask yourself what this moment is trying to teach you. Either you can let worry about the future send you into a spiral, or you can get curious about what this moment is trying to show you.

You can fall into the tomorrow trap.
Or let today be your teacher.

Every time the tomorrow trap is looming, a lesson is also waiting close by. The panic is a sign that you're holding on to something a little too tight—a belief, a fear, an insecurity. You just have to learn to ask yourself good questions and let the moment teach you: *What's going on beneath the surface? Why did that anniversary dance make me panic? Why is my mind spiraling out of control? Why did I just trade in logic for panic?*

"Longer than fifty years?" A few couples remained standing, expertly swaying in each other's arms, decades of practice on full display.

I watched from table 13.

Today is my teacher.

My short breaths got longer. My heartbeat got slower. I felt myself coming back to the present moment, and as I did, I realized this moment had something to teach me. It was training me how to celebrate other people's relationships without panicking about not having one. It was showing me how to be happy about other people's timelines instead of comparing them with mine.

Have you ever noticed how different our ideal timelines are from reality? As the old saying goes, we make plans, and then God laughs at them and makes us wait a lot longer. (Is that how it goes?)

Those two extra hours of silence from that person you're interested in.
Those two extra days you spent waiting for a response after you put yourself out there.
Those two extra years of singleness when you wanted to be in a relationship.
Those two extra decades of living alone when you desired to be married like the rest of your friends.

With each solo trip around the sun, your odds of ever winning the anniversary dance seem to prance away.

But timelines cause tension only until we surrender them. Until we let go of our agenda and focus instead on what we can learn along the way. *Will this situation be resolved by the end of the day? I don't know, but I'm ready to be fully present and experience whatever the day brings, because today is my teacher.*

When you feel like your entire world is in limbo, when you're tired of here and just want to be there . . . *today is my teacher.*

When you get rejected again and start to worry that this pattern is going to continue forever . . . *today is my teacher.*

When you have a broken heart and can't imagine a day when the pain will ever be gone . . . *today is my teacher.*

"Sixty years?" the DJ finally said. One couple remained. The rest of us let out a collective *awwww* as we stood and erupted in well-deserved applause.

The tomorrow trap tries to convince you to check out and trade in presence in the moment for panic about the future. Unfortunately, when you give in, you miss out on everything today has to teach you. A six-decade marriage between people who have chosen love through the highs and lows, in sickness and in health, who have decided that their commitment to each other is more important than feelings or circumstances, isn't something to be jealous of. It's something to marvel at. It isn't something to envy. It's something to enjoy.

To learn from.
To be inspired by.
To stand up and applaud.

Overcome the tomorrow trap, and you'll begin to notice that life is full of those moments.

And that's great and all, but you may still be wondering how you should answer someone next time they ask you if you have the gift of singleness.

Seriously, Though, Do You Have the Gift?

"Do you have the gift of singleness?"

If you've ever had a single person flinch and react to the question instead of responding, here's what's happening. It's hard for us to think about that question without falling into the tomorrow trap. If we admit that we have the gift or that we don't hate being single, at some level we think that means we'll be single for the rest of our lives.

The tomorrow trap strikes again, this time reminding you that your singleness is a curse from God, which means you'd better get used to this loneliness because you're going to feel it for the rest of your life. Of course, that's not true, but the tomorrow trap looks for any opportunity to make you worry.

Singleness feels like anything but a gift at the moment someone
asks you about it, right? It feels like a trap. Like the walls are closing in and time is running out. And of course, like I said earlier,
the question they're really asking is "Are you going to be single for
the rest of your life?" Which misses a massively important truth
about reality.

I don't know!
How could I?

The rest of my life? That's (hopefully) a long time. I'll be honest: I
don't even know what I'm going to have for dinner tonight.
Sometimes we treat God like a fortune teller. We act like we start
following Jesus on Sunday and then on Monday there's a three-
ring binder on our desk labeled YOUR NEXT SIXTY YEARS.

Here's where you're going to live.
Here's what you're going to do.
Here's who you're going to marry.
Here's how many kids you're going to have.

And here's the angel Gabriel's number. If you need any clarification
on anything, just call him, and he'll be right there to clear up any
uncertainty about your future.

Yet Jesus said things like "Don't worry about tomorrow."[2]

I don't believe he was giving an impossible command.

True contentment isn't reserved for eternity.

Abundant life is available to you today—here and now.

So I have a plan for that question. When people ask me if I have
the gift of singleness—if I like being single and if I'm going to be
single for the rest of my life—here's what I say: "My singleness is

a gift." It's funny how the right word can help get my heart in order.

Think about how many advantages there are to being single. Since you're single, do you know what you get to do with your money? Spend it how you want. Do you know what you get to do with your room? Decorate it (or don't) the way you want. Do you know what you get to do with your time? Fill it with whatever activities you want.

That may sound cheap to you. Like decorating how you want is a lame substitute for finding the love of your life. But that's the whole point. Every season of life has advantages and disadvantages. The goal is to have gratitude for what you do have instead of ruminating on what you don't have.

Will I be single for the rest of my life? I don't know. But I, like Paul, believe that singleness provides a huge advantage. And instead of using my extra time, resources, and space to cope with the disadvantages of being single, I choose to take advantage of the advantages.

Marriage is a gift, but so is singleness. So, instead of seeing marriage as the ultimate goal and just trying to survive until I get there, I choose to thrive right here.

These days the only interest I have in the tomorrow trap is the information I can glean from falling into it every once in a while. When that happens, I stop, breathe, get curious about what I need to surrender, and then smile and thank God for this moment because singleness is a gift, and so is today.

The first time I realized this was in Hawaii.

What Hawaii Taught Me
"Why?"

That's my friend Matt's favorite question. Remember him from that trip I can't stop talking about? The one who told me about all the ones that got away? He's been one of my best friends since we played in a highly ambitious, minimally talented band we started in middle school called Chasing Rabbits. For a while there, we were all the rage. And when I say "rage," I'm referring to the anger of Matt's neighbors, which had them repeatedly calling the cops to shut down the "concerts" we'd play in his garage.

Matt's wife is from Hawaii, so after he hung up the sticks, he moved out there with her and became a counselor—a really good one. Mostly because he mastered the art of asking the same question little kids ask on repeat: "Why?"

I have a rule for life: When your friend has a house in Hawaii and you have an open invite, don't be rude; visit often.

During one of my visits, Matt and I spent a day at a spa in a ritzy club right off the coast. At the end of a day of saunas, cold plunges, and delicious food, we sat down by the pool and watched the sun set over the sea after an afternoon storm. We sipped our drinks as kids gleefully splashed in the shallow end, parents gladly letting them tire themselves out before heading home. To the east, a giant well-kept lawn and rolling hills looked like they belonged in the Shire. To the west, the ocean. The storm was now gone, leaving nothing but the smell of rain in the air and a few clouds for the sun to paint a picture on as it set—blank canvases for the evening entertainment.

Basically, the Garden of Eden.

(Is that a detailed enough description? I could keep going, but that might not be helpful. After all, we're trying to practice being content and present today where we are.)

The view was spectacular. The weather was perfect. And the sunset was gorgeous. But the conversation is what I remember most:

M: "Why don't you like to talk about your singleness?"
R: "I guess I just don't think it's all that interesting."
M: "Why?"
R: "I don't know. People love *love*."
M: "And you think that disqualifies your story?"
R: "I mean, I guess. It makes me feel like I'm showing up to the potluck empty-handed."
M: "Do you worry about that a lot?"
R: "All the time."
M: "Why?"
R: "I don't want to be that guy."
M: "What guy?"
R: "The out-of-touch guy. Look, singleness is fine for me now, right? It's kind of unique. But that has an expiration date on it. I feel like I'm going to just become more and more boring, more and more irrelevant."
M: "Why?"
R: "All my mentors are married. The guys I look up to all chose that path. I feel like I'm moving forward in the dark. I'm just too logical. I can't stop thinking about where this path is heading. Like rushing water heading toward a waterfall."
M: "Can you change direction?"
R: "I don't want to change direction. I just want there to not be a waterfall."
M: "Because the waterfall represents . . ."
R: "Being an irrelevant, selfish, socially awkward single person who only cares about himself."
M: "I mean, you see why that's not really rational, right? You

will keep getting older, but you get to decide who you want to be when you get there."

R: "It doesn't feel that way. It feels inevitable. I don't like the future version of myself."

M: "Why?"

R: "Because the future me doesn't know he's worthy of love."

M: "Well, you are worthy of love. And so is the future you. Do you believe that about yourself?"

Pause for tears.

Matt was probably skipping through about three sessions of counseling, but I wasn't paying for any of it, so I couldn't complain. I didn't even buy the drinks.

There's the truth about today.
And then there's the tomorrow trap.

The truth about today is that I'm loved, valued, and accepted right where I am. But it's awfully hard for me to see that and even harder for me to believe that because, most of the time, I'm caught up worrying that there's a time limit on that love. *Well, that may be true today, but give it another five years, and it won't be true anymore.*

Tick-tock.
Tick-tock.
Tick-tock.

I thought the future version of myself needed to be married to know he's worthy. Irrational? Of course. But that's what happens when you don't take time to still the water in your soul. Rough water is so murky that it's tough to see the tomorrow trap lurking in the bushes, getting ready to pounce.

The tomorrow trap had me so tied up in its twisted scheme that it took a breathtaking view, a gorgeous sunset, and a worthy conversation with a good friend to wiggle out of its clutches.

The truth is, I'm good right where I am. I'm loved, valued, and accepted today. Tomorrow? Well, by the time I get to tomorrow, that will be today, and the same thing will be true about me whether I'm single, dating, engaged, or married. Matt's questions were helping me realize that I'm fully covered no matter where I am. It just took Hawaii for me to see it.

"All your mentors may be married, but have you ever thought that there are probably a lot of people younger than you searching for someone to look up to?"

"It's a fair point. That's what the majority of my pastoral meetings end up turning into."

"Maybe you could write about that."

"I don't know, man," I said, taking a healthy sip of my drink. "Do you really think anyone wants to read a book written by a single guy?"

"It seems like you're saying that's the book you wish you had."

Whatever, Matt.

As we got up to leave, I noticed the pool had cleared out. Without the kids splashing, the water was so still I could see the bottom. It was one of those fancy pools where the bottom was layered with tiny pebbles. Each one glistened in its own unique way in the final rays from the setting sun.

Rough water is impossible to see through.
Still water brings clarity.

The tomorrow trap was keeping the water in my soul so turbulent that I couldn't see clearly. It was turning my wonder into worry and making me second-guess tomorrow. *Is there something wrong with me?* As Matt and I talked, my soul and the pool were experiencing the same phenomenon—rough water becoming still. And the stillness brought with it a new clarity, a new perspective, exposing the tomorrow trap for the lie that it is.

Ever since that moment, I've been searching for ways to still the water. It's not always easy. The world has all sorts of tactics to try to keep the water rough in the single's soul: Romantic comedies teach us we're missing out, anniversary dances at weddings remind us we're running out of time to feel the rush of winning, churches skip right over singleness and devote entire sermon series to dating and marriage, and marketers spend billions trying to convince us there's something wrong with us.

If we want to be content while being single today, we have to start naming those tactics and practice finding stillness amid the storm.

That's what the rest of part 2 is about, starting with the scariest enemy a single person faces. The enemy that's undefeated. The one we all try to outsmart but have only managed to push back temporarily. The one that gives us wrinkles, steals our hair, slows our metabolism, puts bags under our eyes, and makes single people panic.

It's time to talk about *time*.

Chapter 6

Bring the Wine

Outsmart the Shot Clock

"Two and a half . . ."
"Two and a quarter . . ."

When Doug and I were kids, we spent every free moment playing basketball. Growing up with a brother I was close with meant I always had someone else to compete against. Even when all the other neighbor kids were busy, we'd be out on our driveway playing intense games of one-on-one.

We'd compete all day, and when our dad got home from work, he'd want to jump in and join.

But of course, when you're in the middle of a heated game, the last thing you want to do is stop and add a third. Some dads would have waited until their sons finished a game, but ours took a different approach.

He'd walk up the driveway and shout, "Five, four, three . . ."

At that point, whoever had the ball would panic. We'd seen *Space Jam* enough times to know what was happening. Time was running out. It was now or never. This was the moment to jump from half court and win the game.

"Two and a half . . ."
I'd try to cross my brother over and get a good look.

"Two and a quarter . . ."

"Two . . ."

And then, all out of options, I'd summon my inner Hakeem Olajuwon, heave up a hook shot, say a quick prayer, and hope for the best.

It took me several years to realize my dad's counting didn't hold any authority—it wasn't real. There were no refs, no clock, no reporters from ESPN ready to ask me how I managed to make that final shot. Just a dad who wanted our game to end so he could join.

Brilliant move. More power to him.

I talk to single people all the time who are on edge about their relationship status. Like they have a shot clock counting down in their head. Like God is up in heaven, pulling the same move my dad used on my brother and me. He's got Gabriel on the loudspeaker yelling, "Five, four, three . . ."

One of the tomorrow trap's main strategies is to taunt us. To tell us there's something wrong with us and we're running out of time to fix it. I wonder if that's why there's inherent anxiety baked into singleness—a subtle but consistent drip of worry that never stops splashing down on the single's soul.

"Two and a half . . ."

"Two and a quarter . . ."

But of course, there are two problems with shot clocks. The first is that they force you to settle for shots you wouldn't typically take, and the second is that they make it really hard to relax and be yourself.

After all, you're on the clock.
You'd better impress.

You'd better make your move.
Time is running out.
Take your shot.

The shot clock adds a lot of pressure. Some of it is self-imposed, coming from within. But an awful lot of it is coming from without. It's coming from every movie you watch, show you binge, and billboard you see. It's coming from every Instagram post of a happy couple you scroll by. And it's coming from all your well-meaning friends and family.

A few years ago, I was golfing with a single friend who told me he wasn't excited to go home for the holidays. Not because he doesn't love his family, not because they don't mean well, but because he's tired of getting the same old questions about his love life, the same old comments about what he's doing wrong, and the same old pep talk about how much happier he'll be when he finds someone.

Because, apparently, it's impossible to love life without a love life.

Ring by Spring

In those days, when I wasn't sitting in empty church parking lots, officiating weddings, or complaining in Bill's office, I was usually trying to learn. I had fallen in love with the Bible, theology, and spiritual formation and had an unquenchable appetite for more knowledge. I started teaching midweek classes at the church where I'd walk people through the Bible, talk about prayer, try to explain other world religions, and cover anything else I could think of.

I decided if I was going to keep teaching, I should probably continue learning. I enrolled in a seminary down the street called Talbot School of Theology and started taking night classes, working toward getting a master's degree. The school was amazing. And besides a few obligatory "I'm walking away from my faith" moments (a topic for another book), I loved the experience. I especially liked the time I got to spend having conversations with my peers.

One evening, around the time that anniversary dance thrust me into the tomorrow trap, I was walking across the quad with one of my classmates, talking about atonement theories (as you do when you're in seminary).

He was a retired pastor on a mission to never stop learning. The guy was brilliant. Stern—but brilliant.

It was a beautiful fall evening. The sun was going down, the weather was perfect, and the lawn was littered with students. Talbot is a small branch of a school called Biola, which has a massive undergrad program that checks every box of a stereotypical Christian college. Some people were throwing Frisbees, some were slacklining, and one guy was playing his guitar with his shirt off.

You know, college stuff.

Out of nowhere, my (typically very serious) colleague elbowed me, pointed to the students, and said, "Ring by spring." Then he just chuckled to himself.

My undergrad experience at the University of Colorado Boulder was very different from Biola, so I had no idea what that phrase meant. Thinking it was some deep theological statement, I asked him to elaborate, and he looked at me like I was the super out-of-touch kid who wasn't a part of the in-crowd like he was.

"Every year," he explained, "these fall evenings are where college kids pair up. They fall in love, and then they want to have sex. But they can't. At least, not without feeling heaps of shame. And so, instead, they save up all their money to buy a ring by spring."

As he was talking, I looked around and realized atonement theories weren't the only thing he was an expert on. He was right. There was a nervous energy across the field. As if time was running out to solidify who they were going to spend the rest of their lives with.

"Two and a half . . ."
"Two and a quarter . . ."

908 Bottles of Wine

Jesus was single but never seemed to be in a hurry.

He wasn't rushed. He never appeared to be on edge. And apparently, he didn't have a shot clock ticking down in the back of his mind. Because when he got invited to drop everything he was doing and walk more than eight miles to go to a wedding in Cana, he said yes.[1]

Jesus was single, but he was also a big fan of weddings.
And he was a big fan of marriage.

We may have the capacity to be with lots of people, but God offers a higher human calling to commit to one person for life. And Jesus saw marriage not only as God's plan for human flourishing but also as a symbol of the covenant love God has for us. In other words, getting married is a beautiful way to be a picture of a God who went to great lengths to show his love to his people.

So it's only fitting that the vows should be accompanied by a giant party.

In the first century, weddings were massive celebrations. I'm sure you've been to a few good weddings, but some of these parties two millennia ago lasted seven days. You'd think a guy who was starting a movement to change the world would be a little too busy to walk over eight miles and dance for a week. You'd think he'd have known that the shot clock was winding down, his journey to the cross was only a few short years away, and he still had a whole lot to accomplish.

"Two and a half . . ."
"Two and a quarter . . ."

But the shot clock didn't have any power over Jesus. The tomorrow trap wasn't holding his happiness hostage. So, when Jesus got invited to the wedding, he went.

When he arrived, his mother informed him that whoever was in charge of ordering the drinks had made a massive mistake. They severely underestimated the crowd (maybe because they weren't expecting Jesus and his disciples to show up), and it wasn't long before they ran out of wine.

Running out of wine may not seem like that big of a deal to you, but it was a huge deal to the master of the banquet. (Which is what they called the wedding planner in the first century. I vote we bring that one back.)

Imagine running out of wine on day one of a seven-day celebration.

That would've been the talk of the town for weeks. Again, not the biggest deal compared with the scope of everything Jesus was up to, but one of the things the life of Jesus shows us is that God cares about the little things. If it's important to us, it's important to him.

So Jesus stepped in and performed the very first of his miracles ever recorded. He assembled a team and had them fill six massive jars that held twenty to thirty gallons apiece.

By the way, if you read the story, it doesn't just say they filled the jars; it says "they filled them to the brim."[2] I wonder if that detail is there for a reason.

Six jars. Twenty to thirty gallons each. Each one filled to the brim. I'm not a numbers guy, but even I know that means we're dealing with 120 to 180 gallons of water.

And then Jesus turned all that water into wine.

For some reason, I used to read that story and picture a few bottles. But let's do a little math (not my specialty).

One gallon equals 3.7854 liters.

And 180 gallons equals 681.372 liters.

Since one bottle of wine is .75 liters, we're talking about 908 bottles of wine.

That's a lot of wine.

And quite a way to show up to a wedding.

John Eldredge pointed that number out in his phenomenal book *Beautiful Outlaw* to show that Jesus lived a life of extravagant generosity.[3]

I've always held on to that example because I've been to a lot of weddings by myself. And going to a wedding by yourself can be awkward. You feel out of place, like being the only one at a costume party who didn't get the memo. Especially when you spend the entire anniversary dance sitting alone at table 13. When you feel that way, it's easy to focus all your energy and attention on yourself and make the night about how you don't have a special someone, instead of making it about celebrating that your friend found theirs.

If you're a fan of *The Office*, think Michael Scott at Phyllis's wedding.[4]

So I love how practical Jesus's first miracle was. He showed up ready to serve and prepared to celebrate. The event wasn't about him, and he didn't try to make it about him. It almost feels like it was a wink to all the single people. Like Jesus was giving us a practical blueprint for how to show up to a wedding:

> Don't bring the spirit of envy.
> Bring the spirit of celebration.
> Don't bring a dark cloud.
> Bring the wine.

Plus None

Remember that night my friend asked me if I had the gift of singleness and I got insecure about it? Something else was going on at that time, adding to the insecurity. All my friends were getting married. My friends like to do everything at the same time, including proposing and getting married, so I was a groomsman in four weddings in a single summer.

I lived in California, and they lived in Colorado, so I used all my vacation days and spent any extra money I had flying back and forth, attending bachelor parties, and buying whatever outfit they asked me to wear.

It was extremely fun.
And expensive.

Each wedding was special for its own reason. I got to stand up with my best friends and support them as they committed their lives to their wives.

But then there was this other thing in the air. A feeling that's difficult to explain. In the middle of all the celebrating, I felt a nervous energy. I didn't have words for it at first, but I heard Bill's voice in my head, telling me to give it a name. So I gave it my best shot:

> *Wait. My friend is announcing to the world that I'm no longer*
>   *his best friend?*
> *Am I being replaced?*
> *I wonder if our friendship is going to change?*
> *My friends are all getting married, and I haven't been on a*
>   *date in two years.*
> *Should I be more concerned about this?*
> *Is there something wrong with me?*

Weddings illuminate just how single a single person is, especially when the plus one is always a plus none.

When another married couple shows up at a wedding, they're celebrating that their friends are entering the same life stage as them. They get to enjoy the night, knowing they'll soon have even more in common with the couple.

But when a single person shows up at a wedding, they're celebrating that their friend is graduating from the same life stage as them and heading into a new one. So, as happy as they are for their friend, there is this nagging thought in the back of their mind that they're about to have less in common.

It's a strange experience. And fertile ground for the tomorrow trap.

That's one of the reasons some people feel off at weddings. That's one of the reasons the evening can be such a roller coaster of emotion. That's one of the reasons some toasts have those uncomfortable, passive-aggressive, "I'm not sure that last thing was a joke" moments. That's one of the reasons some people end up carrying a dark cloud with them disguised as a smile.

And one of the reasons other people end up drinking way more than they planned.

Because your friend is accomplishing something amazing: They're getting married. They're moving forward in life. Which is incredible for them, but it's also (unintentionally) holding up a mirror to you, reminding you that you aren't there yet.

You're falling behind.

And the shot clock is ticking.

"Two and a half..."
"Two and a quarter..."

Falling Behind

When my friend asked me about the gift of singleness that Sunday evening, I didn't respond securely; I reacted insecurely. I didn't know it at the time, but looking back, I see it was because, with every wedding, I felt like I was falling a bit further behind.

If we took a massive survey of all the single people in the world and asked them to make a list of the things they lose sleep over, we'd have quite a compilation of greatest hits. It'd be full of fears, failures, and frustrations. But I'd bet we'd spot a pattern. I'd wager my next paycheck that most of the items would fit into a category labeled I FEEL LIKE I'M FALLING BEHIND.

Wait. All my friends are getting engaged? I haven't been on a date in months. . . . I feel like I'm falling behind.

Now they're buying their first home? I'm still struggling to pay rent. . . . I feel like I'm falling behind.

They set a date? I don't even have a plus one to take to the wedding. . . . I feel like I'm falling behind.

They're already having kids? All my relationships seem to end the same way. . . . I feel like I'm falling behind.

Single people aren't the only ones who feel the pressure to keep up with others; every human does at some level. But from my own experience and hundreds of conversations, I've noticed over the years that single people carry an extra, unique "I feel like I'm falling behind" weight.

For me, when I'm progressing in other areas of my life, the weight isn't all that heavy. When my career is moving forward, the church is growing, and my calendar is full, the weight is no big deal.

But when things slow down . . . different story.

Here's a paragraph I wrote back in 2020, at the beginning of the pandemic: "For the last few years, I've been busy building a church with some of my best friends. Every week, we create space for people to meet together and experience God. However, at the moment, we aren't allowed to do that. Currently, things aren't moving up and to the right. For the last two years, I've never reached the end of my to-do list. Today, I did. So, now what?"

Do you know that feeling? That sinking sensation in the pit of your stomach because you think you're falling behind? That feeling that there's a monster in your soul that you've been able to keep at bay with a full schedule and success but now you're quickly running out of weapons to fight it off? Which means you have to either run away or face it head on.

"Two and a half . . ."
"Two and a quarter . . ."

It's Already Yours

Why wasn't the shot clock a problem for Jesus? Why didn't the tomorrow trap plague him? Or, more accurately, how did Jesus become so accustomed to it that it didn't dictate how he lived?

That's the million-dollar question, isn't it? If we can answer it, we'll have a shot at taking Jesus up on his offer to stop worrying about tomorrow and thrive being single today. So here goes my best attempt to put all these pieces together and give you an answer. Hopefully, it's worth the money you paid for this book. (But, hey, if it's not, you could always return it.)

In Luke's gospel, there's a scene where Jesus told three consecutive stories to a bunch of religious leaders who were very much caught up in the fear that they were falling behind.[5] They even called themselves the Pharisees (which comes from the Hebrew word *parush,* meaning "one who is separated").[6] Nothing says, "Oh man, I really hope I'm okay," like naming yourself "the one who is separated and doing better than everyone else."

Few things bring out the competition in people faster than religion.

All three stories were about someone who lost something, found it, and then threw a party. The first two were about losing a sheep and a coin, but the third story was the real knockout punch. It was about a loving father who watched his son take his inheritance early and leave home. But when the son returned, his father was overcome with emotion, ran out to welcome him, and threw him a party. The father busted out the band, the best food, and the choice wine, and they celebrated.

Except one person didn't join the party.

The father had another son, the older son, who had never left home and was furious that they were throwing a party for his lawless, impulsive brother. Instead of grabbing some wine and joining in on the fun, the older son sat out in the field and watched.

Where's my party? I've been working hard every day for years, so why don't I get a celebration?

The older son thought he was winning the race. Every day his younger brother was out being reckless, he figured he was pulling further and further ahead in the standings.

But then he saw his father hug his brother, give him a robe and the family ring, and throw him a party.

Do you see why this could've been a frustrating moment for that older brother?
Do you see how all-consuming this competition mindset can be?
And do you see how Jesus was masterfully inviting a bunch of religious people to stop playing the game that God never intended for them to play in the first place?

Listen to the father's wise words to his older son: "My son, . . . you are always with me, and everything I have is yours."[7] Which makes me wonder if the reason we feel like we're falling behind is that we haven't yet fully realized that God is always with us and that everything he has is ours.

The father dropped that line, and then the story ends. As the older son stood on the edge of the party, hearing the invitation to come in and celebrate, the screen fades to black. We never hear if he went in.

Because, like any good story, this one was less about finding out what happened and more about holding up a mirror to the religious leaders (and you and me) so they could examine their own souls.

The Eternal Reception

This brings us back to those summer weddings in Colorado. The ones where a part of me was ready to celebrate my friends, and another part was not. A part of me was fully embracing the future, and another part still had a death grip on the past. A part of me was celebrating, and another part was out in the field. A part of me was at their wedding, and another part was at my own pity party. A part of me was dancing, and another part was mourning. A part of me was content being single today, and another part was too caught up worrying about tomorrow.

Because a part of me fully believed God when he said, "You are always with me, and everything I have is yours." And another part did not.

The only way to embrace being single today is to be honest about the parts of you that are stuck worrying about the future. The parts of you that aren't ready to go into the party today, because you want to keep working for tomorrow. We all have these parts.

The only way to move past those insecurities is to learn to outsmart the tomorrow trap. The shot clock may be real and time may be moving forward, but Jesus understood a secret: We may be getting older, but we're going to live forever. We may be marching toward the grave, but there is resurrection on the other side of it. You may be longing for your wedding day, but that day is merely a shadow of something bigger.

In the final two chapters of the Bible, we get a glimpse of the end, the place this whole thing is heading toward. And the primary image is a wedding between heaven and earth.

The ultimate wedding. Where heaven and earth are unified again—together forever. The celebration that ensues will make a seven-day reception look tame because this one will never end.

"Two and a half . . ."
"Two and a quarter . . ."
"Two and . . . Oh, wait. It doesn't matter, because time isn't finite."

The reception will be one for the books. We'll toast, we'll dance, we'll laugh, and we'll probably wonder why we wasted so much precious energy worrying about falling behind in a competition that was never actually happening. Because as it turns out, God has always been with us, and everything he has is ours.

During his years of ministry, Jesus was a picture of this final wedding. He was a pocket of heaven present on earth. Wherever Jesus went, heaven went with.

Think about it: Whenever Jesus showed up, blind eyes opened, demons left, sinners were seen, and relationships were restored. It was the kingdom of heaven on earth. Jesus was a walking wedding celebration!

Maybe that's why when some people asked him why his disciples weren't fasting, he responded, "How can the guests of the bridegroom fast while he is with them?"[8]

Weddings aren't a time for fasting—they're a time for eating cake. And for those special years when Jesus walked around in the flesh, he took the wedding with him wherever he went. He knew that once he left, fasting would once again become an essential spiritual discipline that would help his followers reconnect and remember. But while he was with them, it was time to eat, drink, and dance.

I wonder if Jesus was giving us a practical example of how to out-smart the tomorrow trap.

Do you want to be content being single today? Start by under-standing where we're heading—the ultimate wedding celebration of heaven and earth coming together. It turns out, tomorrow is a trap only when you're thinking too small about it. If you think far enough into the future, you realize what awaits us is an eternity of friendship and joy in the new heavens and the new earth. The temporary future may feel like an enemy to singleness, but when you look at it correctly, you realize it isn't the enemy at all.

One day that celebration will happen in full, but today we can help it happen in part.

How?

By showing up each day the way Jesus showed up to the wedding in Cana—ready to celebrate other people. To be an example of that future reality of unity and joy today.

Instead of competing with others, celebrate them. Instead of ex-pending your energy worrying about the shot clock, spend it cheering others on. Treat their win like it's your win, because their victory doesn't equal your defeat. And their wedding doesn't mean you're falling behind.

In light of eternity, there is no competition—there is no shot clock.

There are just opportunities to celebrate life. Every room you walk into has a person to applaud. Every interaction you have is with someone who wouldn't mind a little encouragement.

You may be single, but there is an eternal wedding in your future. Be a picture of that reality today by carrying a spirit of celebration with you wherever you go.

Stop counting—start commemorating.
Stop competing—start celebrating.

And next time you go to a wedding by yourself, don't bring a dark cloud. Bring 908 bottles of wine.

Chapter 7

Less Grasping, More Laughing

How to Let Go When You Start Overthinking

I don't like horror movies. Honestly, I don't really trust people who do. (That and those serial killer shows. Does your interest in those ever raise any red flags? Because it should.)

I often wonder what the set is like when they film those movies. When the director yells "Cut," what's going on? Are people scared? Are they on edge? Isn't it weird to think about them all sitting around, eating pizza, and laughing?

That's the thing about scary movies. They're trying to cast a spell on people, and as long as you let the spell work, you can stay scared. But as soon as the spell is broken, horror movies become comedies.

What happens when you're home alone at night, watching a scary movie? It's terrifying. Every creaking pipe in your ceiling is a ghost haunting you. And when DoorDash knocks on your door to deliver your Chipotle burrito (with guac because you're single and can afford it), you're certain it's someone coming to murder you.

But when your roommate gets home, their presence changes things, and so does the light they turn on. The spell starts to lift. You look around and realize you're safe. And then another friend shows up, starts watching with you, and points out the giant plot hole, and it makes you laugh.

A scary movie is scary only when it can cast a spell on you. But as soon as you shine a light on what's really happening and begin laughing at the absurdity of the plot, the movie loses all its magic.

Laughter outsmarts scary movies.
It also outsmarts singleness.

Whether you're afraid of being alone or afraid of being in a relationship, there is a solution. There is a way to break the spell. It's the same tactic you use with scary movies: laughter.

Singleness is scariest when you're experiencing it in isolation—like when you're home alone at night, scrolling through Instagram, feeling like you must be the only person experiencing loneliness. But when you invite a few other people into the journey, it's amazing how quickly things change. And then, when you start laughing about singleness, it's like it loses the grip that it has on you.

Singleness is scary only until you learn to laugh about it. That was one of the final lessons Bill taught me.

You're Not the Savior
Lavender wafted through the air again as Bill welcomed me for what would end up being one of our final sessions. Small talk was practically useless at this point—we were almost two years in. No need to break ice that's already broken.

There are days when you go into counseling (or, in this case, spiritual direction) open to wherever the questions may lead. Then there are other sessions where it feels like you're about to word vomit everywhere.

This day was the latter.

I spent fifteen minutes venting to Bill about a situation I was dealing with where I'd told a joke that made a bunch of people laugh.
Except one girl didn't. So then I thought more about the joke and
realized it was kind of mean. Then I started panicking that it was
offensive. On my drive home, I called her to apologize. She said
she wasn't offended, so I hung up and felt relieved for about thirty
seconds until I started worrying that she'd read into that phone
call that I had feelings for her. I always lived on edge that if I ever
led anyone on, they'd walk away from the church because of me. I
thought about calling her back and telling her it wasn't like that.
But then I realized that if I called her twice in a night, she'd think
I really *did* have feelings for her and I was just saying that I didn't.
Instead, I just overthought it for the rest of the week.

(You know, typical young-adult drama that probably made Bill
second-guess what he was doing with his life.)

"Sounds exhausting," Bill said. "Do you always put that much
pressure on yourself?"

"What?" I said, startled. "No, I'm not putting pressure on myself.
It's everyone else who is putting pressure on me."

That made Bill smile, his Jedi senses picking up the scent. "Okay,
do you always feel like other people are putting that much pressure on you?"

"No," I answered honestly. "Only, you know, when I'm doing
things I get graded on."

"Go on."

"I love to play golf," I explained, "but I'm never going to win a
green jacket, so I don't stress out about missing a putt. I love basketball, but I gave up on the dream of playing for the Nuggets
years ago, so I don't worry about missing a shot. The win with

sports is just showing up and playing. Good game, bad game—it doesn't matter. Showing up and having fun is the win."

Bill nodded, a silent invitation to keep talking as my fists tightened.

"But I get a paycheck to pastor, so every interaction in the lobby makes me nervous. If someone is mad at me, I have to do whatever I can to make them feel better. And every time I show up to a party, I need to make sure I'm having fun but not too much fun. I need to show everyone that I care about them and am listening to them, but I can't give any one person (especially a female) too much attention, or they may get the wrong impression. And so, I panic, and then I drive home overanalyzing every word, hoping the jokes were funny but not too inappropriate. Hoping my attention was intentional but not too intentional. Hoping I was having enough fun to show people that pastors can be joyful but not too much fun to the point where people thought I drank too much."

Bill pointed to my hands. I stared down at my shaking fists turning white.

"Just interesting to note how relaxed they were until you started talking about the social situations," he said. "Then they closed. What did you feel?"

I thought about objecting, but I was caught white-handed, so I didn't say anything.

"I don't think you give people enough credit," Bill said bluntly.

"What do you mean?"

"You're a pastor, not a Savior. You're talking to grown adults, not children. They'll be okay. They don't live and die on your every word."

"Maybe that's my problem too. Maybe I'm grasping too tightly to this whole singleness thing."

"Less grasping, more laughing," he said, summing up my rant in four words.

"Less grasping, more laughing," I repeated, more as a prayer than anything else.

Then Bill offered a rare piece of advice. "Maybe this week, you approach all of life the way you approach a round of golf. Knowing that, at the end of the day, there's no pressure. Maybe you walk into every social situation thinking less about how it will impact the future and more about enjoying the present. Maybe you grasp less and laugh more."

"Yeah," I said, downplaying the massive paradigm shift happening in my mind as my hands loosened. "I'll give it a shot."

Less grasping, more laughing.

Since that session in Bill's office, I've adopted those four words as a daily prayer. They don't just turn a horror movie into a comedy; they also transform panic about the future into peace in the present.

Is there a chance that you're grasping on to your singleness? Holding on too tightly to your relationship status? Is there a chance that your death grip on your singleness is keeping you from being open to the new thing God wants to do in your life? Closed hands make it difficult to receive anything new.

The solution to the grasping problem is often to learn how to laugh.

Let Go

When I was five, my brother and I watched *The Mighty Ducks* for the first time—a breakout nineties movie about a peewee hockey team who overcame all odds and won the Minnesota state championship. And then, in the sequel, they suddenly found themselves representing the entire country in the Junior Goodwill Games. A bit of a jump if you ask me, but it's like I've always said: There's no plot hole a few well-placed knuckle pucks can't overcome.

Doug and I were enamored.

The next day, we demanded that our dad take us to the ice rink so we could learn how to skate. I couldn't wait to get on the ice . . . until I got out there and realized how challenging it is to skate when you're barely old enough to run.

"Waterfalls" by TLC blasted through the ice rink's cheap PA system as skaters of all ages and skill levels made their way counterclockwise around the rink. Meanwhile, I was grasping the boards (the wall around the ice), slowly making my way around, terrified of falling.

"There are two ways to approach this, Ryan," my dad said, skating up to me and spraying me with some ice. "You can grasp these boards and slowly and safely make your way around the outside. Or you can head straight into the middle."

Then he smiled and skated off. He knew what he was doing. He knew option one was safer but option two was more effective.

I took the hint. I stopped grasping the boards and headed into the middle. Two things happened that day:

1. I fell a lot.
2. I learned how to skate.

Breakups

Around the time I had that session with Bill, I got caught in the middle of an all-out roast about my singleness. I was eating lunch with four friends, and what started as a simple joke turned into thirty minutes of shots being fired. Being on the wrong side of a roast is a helpless feeling. It's like being strapped into a roller coaster you don't want to be on. You feel it climbing the lift hill, and then at some point, it goes over the top, and there's no turning back.

At that point, there are two options: You can put your head down and latch on to the safety bar with a death grip, or you can let go and enjoy the journey—you can grasp, or you can laugh.

That day, I chose to grasp.

Later that evening, I hung out with my buddy Jimmy who had gone through a breakup earlier that day. (Calling it a breakup is generous. He went on a few dates with a girl, and then she called it off. I feel like the phrase *breakup* is reserved for couples or something. But hey, I'm not writing a dating book. I know nothing about it, so whatever.) Jimmy was going through a breakup.

Jimmy is incredibly sentimental. He wants to be married so badly—has since long before we became friends. He has plans too. Songs picked out for the reception. Ideas to make it special. When he meets that lucky lady, he's going big.

Jimmy thinks about marriage a lot, which is funny since I don't think about it at all. He was having a bad day because he had just lost a relationship. I was having a bad day because I felt like everyone was trying to force me into one. I pointed the irony out to Jimmy. He didn't laugh.

Today I see something that I didn't see back then. If either of us had had any EQ at the time, we would've realized we both had the same problem. We were both having bad days for the same reason—we were holding on too tight.

Jimmy was holding on too tight to the idea of marriage.
I was holding on too tight to the idea of singleness.

Bill wasn't there, but if he had been, I assume he would've told both of us the same thing: "Less grasping, more laughing."

Recurring Nightmares

Have you ever had a recurring nightmare? The type where you wake up in the middle of the night in a pool of sweat. Where you have to take a few deep breaths and get your bearings. And then you start to be so thankful that it was just a dream.

What is the common theme in your nightmare? Drowning? Being chased by clowns? Falling? Death?

I have two recurring nightmares. The first one is relatable to normal people: It's my turn to preach, but I have nothing prepared. So, I slowly walk up onstage and try to get the audience to cheer over and over again while I think up my next move, but nothing comes. Pretty normal. You've probably had your own version of it.

The second one may be harder to resonate with: I'm dressed in a suit, standing in front of all my friends and family, taking vows to commit the rest of my life to a person I've never met. It's my wedding. Then I wake up in a panic and feel so much relief when I realize it's all just a dream.

I remember experiencing it from a young age—like eight or nine. How ridiculous is that? Many people dream about their wedding day, but very few have nightmares about it.

Which is funny for a couple of reasons.

It took me a while to see the humor in it. I used to wake up sweating, but now I wake up laughing. Because it occurred to me that unless things go terribly wrong, no one is ever going to force me to get married. Marriage is something that you get to decide to step into when you're ready. In other words, if I'm standing up at the altar, it's because I've decided to be there. The thing missing in the nightmare is the whole "falling in love with a person and deciding I want to spend the rest of my life with them" thing.

That nightmare used to render sleep impossible for the rest of the night. These days, when I wake up from that dream, I whisper my prayer: "Less grasping, more laughing." Then I quickly fall right back to sleep.

Permission to Change Your Mind

"Do you ever feel like the world is one big courtroom? And the jury consists of every person you know?" I was talking to my friend Kory in the middle of an empty, run-down pizza parlor on a rainy Thursday afternoon. Besides the one employee, a teenager named Andy, we were the only ones in the shop.

Kory is one of those people who is good at reading between the lines. He's less interested in what you're saying and more interested in helping you understand why you're saying it. Not in that annoying way, but in a helpful way. He was just listening and letting me vent, his questions cautious but with enough edge to keep cutting. But then he asked me if I feel that way about singleness, and suddenly, I felt like I'd been thrown into a scene from *Law and Order*.

He could tell.

"Why do you think you get so defensive about innocent questions about your singleness?"

"Not every question makes me angry," I told him, choosing my words carefully. "It's when people ask me if I think I will be single the rest of my life."

"Because you think you will be?" he asked, heading straight for the wound.

Per usual, I froze. My mind drew a blank. Behind the counter, the teenager traded his apron for a robe and grabbed his gavel, the honorable Judge Andy presiding.

"I . . . I . . . I . . ." I stumbled through an answer, pleading the Fifth and wondering if they served pizza in prison.

Kory just laughed. "You know you have permission to change your mind, right?"

In a former life, I would've rolled my eyes, agreed, and changed the subject.

Instead, I stayed in it. And as I did, I realized something embarrassing—I was grasping on to a belief way too hard. Somewhere along the way, I'd picked up the idea that my job was to have the entire world figured out all the time. As if every word I said was being carved into a stone and locked away in an eternal time capsule that I could never take back.

Harmless small-talk questions about my singleness made me feel like I was on trial, because I felt like I was speaking for fifty-year-old Ryan. And eighty-year-old Ryan.

Meanwhile, Jesus said things like "Don't worry about tomorrow."[1] Or, said differently, "Less grasping, more laughing."

You know you have permission to change your mind, right?

That line was like the sun, melting away years of self-imposed, unrealistic expectations.

"Your answer today can just be yes," he continued.

I took a deep breath.

"Yeah," I said, meaning it for perhaps the first time. "I love being single."

"And if that changes tomorrow?"

"That doesn't make it any less true today," I said, finishing his thought. "I have permission to change my mind."

That may sound obvious to you, but for years, I didn't realize it. I felt like I had to lock in my permanent answer about my relationship status and let everyone know if I was going to be single or married for the rest of my life. The thought of committing to an answer for the next several decades is one of the reasons the topic always terrified me. To bring this chapter full circle, that's why singleness often felt like a scary movie to me.

Remember, singleness, like a horror movie, is scariest when you're experiencing it in isolation.

That conversation at the pizza parlor was the equivalent of my friend Kory walking into the room, turning the lights on, and pointing out the giant plot hole in the horror movie I was watching. It moved me from fear to joy. From grasping to laughing.

Do you have people in your life who will walk into the room you're in and turn the lights on? Have you given those people permission to ask you questions about your singleness and point out plot holes in your life when they see them? Have you invested in their lives enough and gained their trust so that you can have those deeper conversations? It takes time to build real friendship, but it's time well spent.

When the right people ask you the right questions or are simply willing to swap stories and laugh about bad dates and breakups, you realize you don't have to be nearly as scared of your single-ness as you thought.

Isolation keeps us grasping.
Solidarity keeps us laughing.

Learn to Laugh
A relationship is a dance—two people learning to move together to create something greater than themselves.

Imagine the beginning of a wedding reception. The bridal party enters as "Let's Get It Started" by the Black Eyed Peas plays a little too loudly, and everyone stands to cheer for the bride and groom. But then they head to the center of the room and sit with two lawyers to discuss their marriage contract.

I'll take out the trash. You do the laundry.
I'll do the taxes. You take care of the lawn.

That would kill the wedding celebration mood quickly. Because no one uses their hard-earned vacation days, redeems their miles, and gets their suit cleaned to watch two people negotiate a contract. We do it to celebrate two people signing up to dance with each other for the rest of their lives.

But married people aren't the only ones allowed on the dance floor. With our first breath, God invites all of us to the dance. It's just that single people like me tend to start holding on too tight to everything and lose sight of that. We end up sitting at table 13 by ourselves all night, eating Jim's and Nancy's slices of chocolate cake while they celebrate sixty years of marriage during the anniversary dance.

Some of my single friends are grasping too tight to the idea of being in a relationship. They watch their friends get married, and the shot clock consumes them. It fills their minds. Laughter becomes foreign, and then if an opportunity for a relationship does come along, they put too much pressure on it and scare the other person away.

And then there are people like me who tend to grasp too tight to the idea of being single. We learned to love it, but now it's become an identity. It's the thing that makes us different. The thing that helps us stand out. Or the thing that we believe makes us extra spiritual or something.

Singleness makes some of us grasp on to the idea of finding a relationship, and it makes others grasp on to the idea of staying single. Either way, we lose.

Remember that homecoming dance during my freshman year of high school? I wasn't able to enjoy dancing with Jamie because I was too busy grasping on to the idea that I didn't want to hurt anyone. I didn't want to make any empty promises that I couldn't keep. I didn't want to set myself up for an awkward conversation that I didn't know how to have.

I was grasping, and my entire body was letting me know.

I had an opportunity to be present and enjoy today, but I was too consumed with tomorrow. That's what the tomorrow trap does. It tries to sneak into your head and convince you to panic, to grasp.

Maybe we need to take a cue from Jesus and approach singleness the way he approached life: "Seek first his kingdom and his righteousness, and all these things will be given to you as well. Therefore do not worry about tomorrow, for tomorrow will worry about itself."[2]

In other words, less grasping, more laughing.

When that relative asks if you're dating anyone yet and you feel like they're twisting a dagger in your heart? *Go ahead and say what you really want to say, Aunt Polly. I get it. I'm letting the family down.*

That's a sign you're grasping and an invitation to practice laughing.

When your friend gets into a relationship and you smile, celebrate, and listen to the story but deep down you feel threatened? *Oh, come on. Benji got into a relationship before me? Really?*

That's a sign you're grasping and an invitation to practice laughing.

When that co-worker's joke about your singleness makes you want to body-slam him into the ground? *Don't start with me, Mark. I don't care, and I'll knock you out and won't even repent for it on Sunday. I don't care.*

That's a sign you're grasping and an invitation to practice laughing.

Singleness is a gift. Like an X-ray machine revealing to us where we're holding on too tight, where we're grasping and need to learn to laugh. Because grasping is what we do when we're worried about the future but laughing is what we do when we're grounded in today.

So that four-word prayer is the answer to just about every situation we've talked about so far.

Why am I writing this book? Will that make it permanent? What if I change my mind?

Less grasping, more laughing.

I don't care.
I don't care.

Less grasping, more laughing.

"Two and a half . . ."
"Two and a quarter . . ."

Less grasping, more laughing.

And when the water in your soul is so rough you can barely make out anything in it?

Less grasping, more laughing.

I wonder what new possibilities we may make room for if we learn to let go a little bit. You may just find that singleness is a lot more fun. It may even start to feel like a gift. And if you do meet someone, you may find that a significant other makes a better dance partner than a hostage.

Chapter 8

Rediscover Wonder

Where to Find Wonder When You're Single

Do you ever wonder where all the wonder went?

Little children don't have to be told to be in awe of the world; they just are. The stars in the night sky, their first bite of something sweet, or a fire truck driving down the road fills their little minds with wonder. But then, somewhere along the way, we lose it.

Kids think flying in an airplane is an adventure—we can't wait to land. Kids look forward to reading a book before bed that'll light their imagination on fire—we can't wait for them to go to sleep so we can let Hollywood create our imagination for us.

When we're young, we're full of wonder. Over time, the world knocks it out of us.

One of the most beautiful things about romantic love is that it's one of the primary ways humans rediscover wonder (or so it has been explained to me).

The intrigue you feel when you meet someone.
The excitement of searching for ways to spend time with them.
The exhilaration of asking them out.
The thrill of a first kiss.
The joy of saying "I love you."
The nervousness you feel as you scheme up a way to propose.

The expectancy of the wedding.
The magic of watching the person you love walk down the aisle.

All those things have something in common: They are wonderful—full of wonder.

Friends go on dates, and most of the time when I ask them about it, their response is pretty neutral. *"Fine. Fun. Maybe there'll be a second."* But then, occasionally, they say something different. You can hear it in their voice, butterflies fluttering out of their stomach with each word.

The words, the smile, the giddiness.

It's like they're discovering the world all over again. As if their eyes have been opened to just how beautiful life really is. And no matter what the world throws at them, they just don't seem to be too thrown off by anything.

Love is God's great reminder of how wonderful life really is. It's been that way ever since Adam woke up from his nap in the garden and laid eyes on Eve.

Which is great for all of them, but what about us? Where does that leave you and me? Are single people destined to live lives void of wonder? Doomed to never experience awe again?

Yes.

I'm kidding. While just about every romantic comedy would have you believe you are, the fantastic news is that you aren't. There is a way for single people to rediscover wonder; we just have to get a little more creative.

Which is one of the many lessons I learned on my road trip to Yosemite.

Yosemite

"I can hear the birds again," I said.

"What?"

"I said, I can hear the birds again."

"That's cool, man."

That was the conversation I had with Ethan while I was on my way out of Yosemite National Park.

When an opportunity came up for Doug, Ethan, and me to plant a church in Austin, Texas, I said a bittersweet goodbye to the church I was working at in California and got ready to move. But before I left, I wanted to make sure I did something to end that season of my life. When I don't bring chapters to a close, my life ends up feeling like one long run-on sentence.

Or at least that's what Bill told me in our last session. I gave him a hug and thanked him for all the help. Then I borrowed a tent from my friend Tyler and drove north. I didn't really know where I was heading. My plan was to drive for a while, surf for a while, find a place to camp, and then repeat.

So, I set out with no plan but to process. Fortunately, if you've ever made that drive, you know it makes processing really easy. Malibu, Carpinteria, Santa Barbara, Pismo, San Luis Obispo, Big Sur—the list goes on and on.

Beaches.
Coffee shops.
Nights under the stars.

It was amazing. Which, of course, is oversimplified. That's how I remember the trip, but when I really stop to think about it, I remember the panic that came on day two when I pulled my car to the side of the road and freaked out about leaving a great job at a great church to move to a city where I didn't know anyone, all to plant a church that nobody currently went to.

I remember the immense loneliness that hit me on day three when I finally got to Yosemite and set up camp. I bought a ham-and-cheese sandwich and sat in front of a fire, missing my friends and wondering what I was out here searching for.

I remember the existential crisis that came on day four when I began to wonder what I was doing with my life. And why I thought I could ever help people connect with this God that I didn't even understand. That day, I hiked up a hill to get some cell service so I could google "how to begin a new career." (By the way, a comforting number of results popped up. It turns out we all ask that question.)

I remember driving into town to get enough cell service to have a two-hour-long conversation with a good friend on day five. She was about to leave her entire life behind and jump headfirst into mission work around the world. A relationship may have worked between us, but neither of us could shake the feeling that we had to follow our own paths—paths that were heading in different directions. I hung up the phone feeling sad, and thankful, and proud of myself for not overthinking every word in the conversation. Less grasping, more laughing!

It's amazing how many thoughts and emotions (both positive and negative) begin to surface when you get away for a few days and give your soul space to be still. The more time I spent on my own, the deeper into my soul I dove, and the more I started to feel. Pain, agony, joy—all of it. They were all playing second fiddle to what I was really feeling: fear about the future.

Most church plants don't even work.
Why did I just quit my job?
Will anyone show up?
Will people want to follow a single pastor?
I have such a good group of friends here. What if I don't meet any-one there?
Is this a bad idea?
What have I done?
There must be something wrong with me.

Processing those thoughts day after day was exhausting. I may've been between church jobs, but feeling all your emotions can feel like a full-time job.

The park's beauty helped, though. If you've never been, it's worth the trip. At first, it feels like any other mountain drive, but then you go through the Wawona Tunnel, and the view on the other side takes your breath away. You see a giant valley, the sun reflecting off the giant mountains. Not just any mountains, but two famous peaks—El Capitan and Half Dome.

El Capitan is famous in the climbing community. That's the one Alex Honnold climbed without ropes in the documentary *Free Solo*. But I'm not a part of the climbing community, so I had my eyes set on Half Dome—aptly named—the massive mountain shaped like a giant dome that got sliced right down the middle during some cosmic battle. It's the crown jewel of the valley.

Every morning, I'd wake up staring at it, feeling like it was calling to me. Like there was something I needed to experience at the top.

Remember, at this point, I hadn't talked to anyone in several days, so if this chapter sounds like I was losing my mind, there may be some truth to that. But every time I looked at Half Dome,

I could've sworn it was staring back at me, inviting me, challenging me.

So, one lazy evening, I went to the store, stocked up on water and PowerBars, and went to bed when the sun went down.

Around 3:00 A.M., my eyes shot open; I knew the day had come. I drove as far as I could, parked my car in a spot surrounded by Beware of Bears signs, and began my hike. There wasn't another soul as far as the eye could see. You feel a kind of solidarity when other hikers are on the trail. It's a reminder that even if a bear attacked, we'd at least go down together.

There was no one, and the sun didn't seem to be close to rising. *Why did I start so early?* It was me versus the mountain. So, I hiked.

And hiked.
And hiked.
And hiked.

Eventually, the first sight of morning light began to creep over the hills. As it did, the mountain came alive. Birds sang, squirrels played tag in the trees, and a black-and-white landscape erupted in color.

I barely noticed. I didn't stop to look. I didn't observe. My mission was to reach the top of the mountain, and I couldn't be bothered.

The trail led me alongside a slow and peaceful stream that became more intense as I climbed. Another half mile, and I could hear a waterfall—alive and active—dumping massive amounts of water into the pool below.

The path beside the waterfall felt more like I was ascending a set of stairs than hiking a trail. At the top, I took a quick glance at the gallons and gallons of rough water rushing over the falls every second—and kept climbing.

Onward.

There was something waiting for me at the top of the mountain. I knew there was. There had to be a reason I'd driven all the way to Yosemite. There had to be a reason I'd woken up so early. There had to be a reason some invisible force seemed to be pulling me out of my tent and up Half Dome.

Onward.

Half Dome, as it turns out, isn't for the faint of heart, and it's not like I'd trained for the journey. I honestly didn't know how long the hike was or if it was even possible to do in one day. The first people I saw all morning were a father and son duo who were just waking up. They told me they'd started the day before because they wanted to take their time.

"Have fun" is what I said. *Losers* is what I thought as I waved and left them in the dust. *Look at me, winning this race.*

Onward.

If you've ever climbed Half Dome, you know it gets a little dicey near the top. Especially in October. The wind picks up, the trail gets narrow, and you end up doing a little light bouldering, which you'd think would be no big deal for a guy who lived in Boulder for several years. But that's where you're wrong. I had more than one "this is where things end for me" moment.

But I made it to the top.

And for the first time in what felt like days, I sat down and exhaled deeply. I grabbed my journal, took out the bar and jug of water I was saving for the top, informed God that I was ready for the divine download waiting for me . . . and waited.

And waited . . .
And waited . . .
And waited . . .

Nothing came.

The view from the top of Half Dome is breathtaking, one of the prettiest places I've ever been, but I couldn't enjoy it. Couldn't sit still long enough to take it all in. No awe; just agony. I sat and stared, wondering how Bill would diagnose my inability to enjoy the moment.

We get weird about mountaintop moments, don't we? We build them up so high in our minds that reality can never hold a candle to our expectations. So, it feels strange to actually get there.

You set your mind on that vacation and circle it on your calendar, knowing that if you can just get there, you'll feel better. But then the day finally arrives—*there* becomes *here.* You lie down on the beach and expect to feel bliss, only to realize you're just as restless as you were back home, now with the added weight of knowing you don't have an upcoming vacation to look forward to.

Or you work your entire life to land a job in a certain field, but then you realize that job has irritating paperwork and infuriating peers like every other job. Two weeks in, you drive home feeling like your dream actually sucks.

Or you just want to be in a relationship, so you work and pray and pursue and fast, and then you finally meet someone, only to realize they're an imperfect person with bad habits and an ability to hurt you. So you break up with them and buy some book about being single today.

A mountaintop always looks more magical from base camp. Once you ascend to the top, it loses some of its luster. Reality lets you down, and you feel foolish for setting such high expectations. You feel duped and wonder why you didn't just spend another lazy day hanging out down in the valley.

Or at least that's what was going on with me.

I was in a bad mood. Scribbling in my journal like a toddler throwing a fit when his father tells him it's bedtime. The logical part of my brain told me to ration my food for the journey down, but the emotional side of my brain vetoed that, and I reached into my bag, needing something to ease the agony. I opened my last PowerBar, wondering why I didn't think to pack a variety of food, and finished it in three bites.

But then something strange happened. Really strange.

On bite number three I felt like I had an out-of-body experience. I'm serious. (Stick with me here. This next paragraph is a little out there, but you've come this far. Trust me—this is important.)

I'd read stories about out-of-body experiences but thought they were silly until I experienced one firsthand. Maybe it was the thin air, or the dehydration, or the fact that the only thing I had in my system was high-fructose corn syrup packaged in what I thought was supposed to be a health bar, but I felt like I left my body and hovered a few feet above my head. I could see myself sitting on top of Half Dome as if my consciousness were a drone that had soared up into the air. Suddenly, I had a third-party perspective on my life. I looked down at myself, staring across the valley, trying to figure out my future. I watched myself scribbling in my journal, working hard to crack life's code.

Look at that guy.
What is he doing?
What is he chasing?
What puzzle is he trying so hard to solve?

That new perspective was what I needed. Something broke. It didn't take longer than a split second for me to start cracking up at the whole scene. This guy was on top of Half Dome, staring at one of the most beautiful sights he'd ever seen, about to enter a new, exciting season where he would get to plant a church with his best friends. And instead of enjoying the view, he was terrified. Panicked. Scrambling to solve the riddle of life.

If that isn't a picture of the problem single people fall into, I don't know what is.

Everything was going great, but I couldn't see it, and I didn't have a person next to me reminding me that we were fine. So I didn't realize it until I got a third-party perspective on the whole situation and was able to observe myself.

Life was good, but one ingredient was missing—surrender.

Surrendering tomorrow is all it would've taken for that unendingly single guy to enjoy the view today. But he was sitting on a rock, overanalyzing everything. Instead of getting lost in the wonder of God's creation, he was outthinking it—grasping instead of laughing.

And that, I realized as I watched myself from above, was the funniest thing I'd ever seen. It was the perspective I needed to see how ridiculous the whole situation was. We put too much pressure on tomorrow, hoping it will fix today. We treat tomorrow like it's holding all the keys to the happiness we're searching for.

Once I finish this class, I'll be at peace.
Once I meet someone, I won't struggle with those thoughts.
Once I get married, I won't worry so much.
Once I get there, I'll feel better about here.

But then you get there, and you realize you are still you.

Same old fears.
Same old insecurities.
Same old struggles.

And that, in a tragic sort of way, is hilarious. And it's the final key to surrendering the future and being present today. Because if we can just swallow that pill, if we can just realize we'll still be imperfect and incomplete when we get there, then we have a shot at being content here.

I caught my breath, looking out at the rolling hills and the afternoon clouds slowly working their way past the peak as the sun descended toward the western sky. For the first time in some time, I felt peace—stillness. The rough water in my soul becoming calm.

I thought there was something waiting for me at the top of Half Dome. A revelation. A brilliant idea. A sermon. A book. A business plan. Instead, the only thing up there was the same invitation waiting in every other moment of life: a beautiful invitation to surrender.

I guess it was the irony that was making me laugh. It took that entire journey to see something that was right under my nose the whole time. Beauty is right in front of us in every moment, with every breath, in every season—wonder is always waiting to be rediscovered.

In heaven, I bet we'll laugh about how uptight we were during our lives and how much wonder we missed while we were racing up the mountain. It may not be our first thought, or even our tenth, but somewhere along the way, we'll sit around a dinner table laughing about how unseen beauty was constantly passing right in front of our eyes. The sunsets, but also all the people we do have in our lives—the friends, the roommates, the neighbors.

Wonder isn't reserved for romantic love; it's available for all of us. It's waiting to be discovered. You just have to put in a little extra time and effort to see it.

Searching for wonder is a bit like excavating artifacts. The wonder is down there; it's just covered up by a lot of pessimism, pain, and fear of the future. If we're willing to slow down long enough, we can carefully wipe away all the stuff that was never meant to be there and let the beauty shine.

When you're single, you have to be a little more proactive to see it.
You have to be a little more intentional to taste it.
You have to be a little more aware to smell it.
You have to be a little quieter to hear it.
You have to be a little more meditative to feel it.

All the magic is there. We just have to get still long enough to experience it.

The Gift of Stillness
The way down Half Dome took me about three times longer than the way up.

I stopped trying to finish the journey and started enjoying it. I wasn't looking down, staring at my next step. I was looking around, taking in everything I could see.

I noticed how much the water picked up speed as it approached the waterfall. Then it sprang into the air like an Olympic diver, whizzed right by me, and splashed into the pool below, then calmed down completely a few seconds later, the raging waterfall now a peaceful stream. The rough and murky water now still. I watched the process for several minutes. As a guy getting ready to step into a new chapter, where there was bound to be some rough water at times, I found the whole progression incredibly comforting.

Squirrels chased each other up and down trees, with seemingly no other agenda but to continue playing the lifelong game of tag they're locked into with their friends.

Then I met a hiker named Greg. I sat down next to him to rest, and he ripped a piece of his sandwich off and shared it with me as he told me about the traveling he'd been doing. He was visiting every national park in the United States. This was number fifty-two. We clinked our water bottles together in a sort of "cheers," and I headed down as he went up.

The birds were out of their nests and singing their songs. I don't know if it was the fact that I hadn't talked to anyone besides the occasional cashier in several days, but as I would later tell Ethan, I could hear the birds. I felt like they were speaking to me. No message. No agenda. Just a reminder that we were all alive. That we were all here. In this present moment.

Slowing down and getting still isn't easy, but you can do it. And don't worry—you don't have to take a solo trip to Yosemite to experience the benefits (unless you want to). You can practice stillness right now as you read this book. Instead of trying to rush to finish this chapter and go on with your day, pause right here in this paragraph, close your eyes, take five deep breaths, and allow yourself to feel any feelings that rise to the surface. Don't judge the thoughts; don't try to change them; just be here now.

How was that experience? What did you notice? What did you feel? If it was uncomfortable, don't feel bad. We live in a world that trains us to always be in a hurry, so practicing stillness is an act of rebellion against a busy world. Sitting in stillness is like using a muscle. If you haven't exercised the muscle much, it may be weak right now, but if you keep working it out, it'll keep getting stronger and stronger.

Along the way, you'll begin to relearn a truth we all knew when we were kids: *The wonder didn't go anywhere; we just need to be still long enough to see it.*

It's so easy to assume wonder is always a day away. It's out there waiting for us at the top of the mountain. We'll find it tomorrow when we finally meet someone, fall in love, or get married. That's a great, God-given avenue for rediscovering wonder. But there's another path. It takes a little bit of work and a lot of surrender, but if you can learn the lost art of stillness and let the rough water in your soul calm down, you can rediscover wonder today.

When you learn how to get still, you realize wonder is always waiting for us. Wonder mocks the tomorrow trap. It meets you on the mountaintop and visits you in the valley. Wherever you are today, wonder is already there waiting. And it turns out, despite popular belief, you don't even need a date to rediscover it.

Which brings us back to Mary of Bethany's story and the second encounter she had with Jesus. In this encounter, tragedy hit. She lost her brother and was faced with the seemingly impossible task of going on without him. Until Jesus showed up and stilled the rough water.

Still the Rough Water

Mary's attempt to lift her head off the tear-drenched floor was unsuccessful. She didn't have the strength, hadn't since her worst fear was realized four days earlier. Her brother—her best friend—was gone.

The tears were but a small picture of the violent storm that raged in her soul.

Guilt.
Anger.
Confusion.
And beneath all of that—hidden in a box she couldn't seem to access—grief.

"Mary," Martha whispered, gently resting her hand on her shoulder with the compassion of the only other person on the planet who understood. "They're on their way. I'm going to go out to meet them."

Mary rolled over and stared at her sister, her face flushed with anguish and anger. Yet she felt a small spark of relief, happy to have something to do after four days of grieving. Everything in her wanted to get up and face the day with her sister, but she couldn't move. The thought of a tomorrow without Lazarus was too much to handle today. She reached deep for words, but the terrible storm thundering in her soul drowned out any meaningful response. Instead, she shook her head and watched her sister leave without her.

Their home was filled with friends and family. Jews from Jerusalem had also come to give their condolences. Her cynical side couldn't help but think they were here to see if Jesus would show up. The last time he was in Jerusalem, he'd barely escaped. Accused of blasphemy, he'd had to retreat across the Jordan River. Showing up here in Bethany, less than two miles from Jerusalem, would be a risk for him and his disciples. But if he'd only shown up four days ago, she knew he could've healed him.

The thought pulsated through her soul, adding power to the wind and rain. Nothing made sense. Nothing was clear. So she didn't get up. Didn't say a word to anyone until her sister returned.

"Mary," Martha said gently but sternly. "The Teacher is here and is asking for you."

Those words lit a fuse. Sorrow turned into rage. *Asking for me? Oh, now he wants to talk to us?* She stood up quickly and walked out of the house, the storm in her soul gathering momentum like an awful hurricane ready to destroy anything in its path. An entourage of mourners followed her as she wound down the trail to the outskirts of town.

"Lord," she practically shouted, reaching Jesus and falling at his feet. "If you had been here, my brother would not have died." Mary didn't recognize herself. It wasn't her talking; it was the frustration. But her typically strong filter was weakened by four days of tears, and the words came rolling out of her mouth before she could stop them.

Jesus seemed to absorb the words, offering no rebuttal. There was deep grief in his eyes as he shared in the pain.

Together they walked slowly and silently to her brother's tomb, the tears streaming down Mary's cheeks with each step. Yet, for the first time in four days, the tears felt acceptable. They felt safe. As if she was in the presence of one who had an endless capacity for them.

Mary hated the stone as soon as she saw it. Hated it to its core. The giant boulder blocked her way—signifying separation from her brother. Unable to go farther, she sat down, and everyone joined her. Wise words or lighthearted humor usually broke the silence within this group, but not today. Instead, it was the sound of weeping. She looked up to see the Rabbi's eyes full of tears. Unashamed, untamed tears. The presence of death stirred something deep within him, almost as if it was a deep reminder that things weren't supposed to be this way.

With each tear he shed, the storm in her soul began to be still. His grief alleviated hers. She took a breath, confusion giving way to clarity, feeling free to face the stone instead of cursing it.

Time meant nothing.
The entire group sat and mourned for what could've been hours. The grief became a friend for Mary. A deep invitation to accept the pain. Ever so slowly, the raging storm in her soul began to still. The wind and the waves became calm, and her thoughts finally became clear.

Jesus, on the other hand, was beginning to shake. He stared intently at the stone in front of him. Mary felt something shift in the air. While her soul was stilling, the Rabbi's was stirring. Silence fell over the group. Everyone's attention was now fixed on Jesus, whose eyes flashed like ferocious lightning in a night sky.

"Take away the stone," he said.

Mary and You

Mary's second encounter with Jesus came in the wake of tragedy. He arrived four days after her brother, Lazarus, died. As you can imagine, Mary was devastated. Life is hard enough when we're surrounded by everyone we love. Facing the future without someone we love is a horrifying reality we all have to experience in our own ways.

Fear of the future is real. It's so real that Jesus sat down and wept right alongside Mary as she tried to process it.[1] He not only gave her space to feel everything but also joined in the pain. The Bible doesn't promise us that nothing is ever going to go wrong, but it does remind us that God will always be with us no matter what happens.[2]

Jesus was giving Mary space to still the rough water in her soul.

Facing the future as a single person feels scary sometimes. But you have to remember that although you're single, you're never alone. Jesus is right by your side, giving you permission to feel, to cry, to get nervous, and to grieve. And then he empowers you to face today with confidence.

For Reflection and Discussion

1. Do you ever have a hard time expressing or feeling your fear of the future? Did you know that Jesus wants to sit in the suffering with you and weep alongside you? What does this story tell you about him? How does it give you confidence to be honest about your own fear?

2. Do you ever notice yourself getting caught in the tomorrow trap? When are you most prone to fall into it?

3. Do you ever feel like you're running out of time to get in a relationship? If so, where (or who) does that pressure come

from? What is one way you can practice releasing yourself from that pressure?

4. Is there something about tomorrow you're grasping on to too tightly? When you start to get anxious about the future, what is one tactic that helps you let go?

5. Does fear of the future ever interfere with potential relationships? Do you find it hard to be present with someone in the moment because you can't stop thinking about the future? If so, why do you think you do that? What would it look like to practice letting go of tomorrow for a day?

PART THREE

Today

This is the day the LORD has made.
We will rejoice and be glad in it.

—Psalm 118:24, NLT

PART 1 WAS ABOUT STIRRING the stagnant water, and part 2 was about stilling the rough water. But there's one more piece to the puzzle.

If stirring the water is the solution for the soul stuck in the past and if stilling the water is the solution for the soul worried about the future, then the only thing left to do is share the water!

Imagine if I were a nutrition coach (I'm not) and you hired me to help you start eating healthier. First we'd sit down and eliminate all the unhealthy food from your diet. But I wouldn't be a very good coach if we stopped there. The whole point in removing the bad is to replace it with the good. Eliminating the unhealthy stuff is the hard part; adding in the healthy stuff is where it gets fun.

In the first two parts of this book, we worked to heal from the past and surrender the future, but all of that was a means to an end. We had to remove all the unhealthy stuff (unforgiveness, worry, etc.) to make room for all the healthy stuff.

Singleness isn't a curse to endure; it's a gift to enjoy. When you aren't spending the whole day being dragged down by yesterday or feeling anxious about tomorrow, you'll notice you have a lot more time to enjoy it.

Here's the trick. You have to make today about something bigger than yourself. Or, to continue our metaphor, once you stir the stagnant water and still the rough water, the final step is to share the water with the world.

Singleness is a gift, and gifts are for sharing. Today you have an opportunity to share your skills with the world. Instead of being stuck in yesterday or consumed by tomorrow, you can make the conscious decision to live for something greater than yourself by being single today!

Chapter 9

The Kingdom of Me

Stop Putting Yourself at the Center of the Story

After that strange out-of-body experience on the top of Half Dome, I was ready for the next chapter to begin. It was time to move to Austin and plant a church. But first I had one more stop on my road trip. One of my favorite Bible teachers was hosting an event back on the coast, a few hours west of Yosemite. The plan for the event was simple—a small room, a whiteboard, and several hours of teaching. My idea of a good time.

I spent a final night under the stars and then packed up my car and headed west. Reentering society after several nights of camping was a rude awakening. The thought of sitting in a room with fifty other people suddenly made me aware of how much I needed a shower. It's funny how other people's presence makes us aware of ourselves.

Sometimes I wonder how much Adam's life changed when he met Eve. Did he ask her to wait outside his home while he threw all the fig leaves back under the tree, picked up the fruit off the floor, and chucked the orange peels out back? (Have I mentioned it's not good for man to be alone?)

The problem was, the event began at noon and every hotel I called wouldn't let me check in until 3:00 P.M. So, I did what any other perpetually single guy would do—I jumped in the ocean. Close enough.

I ducked under the first wave, feeling the freezing salt water wash away the Yosemite dust. The next few waves threw me to the ocean floor and then harmlessly passed by, allowing my body to emerge back to the surface. I struggled to find my breath through chattering teeth while wondering how long I had to be out here for it to count as a shower.

But the next wave that hit wasn't made of water; it was made of nostalgia.

It struck me that I was moving east and that this would be my last time in the ocean for quite some time. I started thinking about how helpful all those sessions with Bill were, how thankful I was for my first pastoral job, and how much I'd learned about my own singleness along the way. Sometimes it's the biggest struggles in life that end up teaching you the most.

And then, right before I surrendered to the cold water and swam back to shore, one last sentimental memory popped into my head. I recalled one of the most memorable surfing moments from my time in California.

It had happened a few years earlier and was memorable not because of the waves but because of the girl standing on the beach.

Take My Picture
The waves weren't great that day. Small. Choppy. Inconsistent. The tide was high, and the evening wind was already howling. Those are all ingredients that keep good surfers away. That's the best part about being a barely mediocre surfer; I care way more about spending time in the water than about how good the waves are. Plus, I'm usually trying to get away from people, so I'll take bad waves over a crowd any day. (Really, Ryan? We hadn't noticed.)

The beach was empty. When I say "empty," I mean there wasn't a single person—no one in the water and no one on the entire beach. No lovebirds walking down the sand complaining about their co-workers. No old guy feeding the seagulls from his chair. No vacationers desperate to brave the wind and get what they paid for.

Empty.

Perfect.

I wasn't planning on staying out long, but then I saw her. A girl around my age walking down the beach with a camera. She stopped right in front of where I was surfing and started watching me intently. I mean, she was staring right at me. And then, in a moment of magic, she set up her tripod and started taking pictures of me.

This is it.

My mind was racing. This was my moment. Remember, the beach was completely empty. If this scene were in a movie, they'd need to cast only two people:

Person 1: beautiful photographer
Person 2: mediocre surfer

A love story for the ages.
She's taking pictures of me.
Oh, did you just ask how we met? Let me tell you a story: The waves weren't great. Small. Choppy. Inconsistent.

My mind formulated the entire plan in a matter of seconds. Ten minutes of surfing, take a wave all the way in, introduce myself, ask to see the pictures over dinner. The rest, as they say, would be history. *God, I don't ask for much. But if you could send a few per-fect waves—the type that makes a below-average surfer look like a slightly above-average one—that would be great.*

The next few moments were magical—poetry in motion. We may have been separated by fifty feet of water, but somehow we just understood each other. Wave after wave. Photo after photo. Two souls falling deeper and deeper into love's spell.

Until I dropped in on the next wave, rode it as long as my skills allowed, and launched over the top to paddle back out. As I did, I looked west toward the horizon, and the view hit my lovesick soul like a ton of bricks. I'd been so focused on the girl to the east that I forgot to look to the west.

I realized in horror that she wasn't snapping photos of me at all. There was actually a strong chance she hadn't even noticed my existence. Because behind me was the most beautiful, epic sunset I'd ever seen. God was showing off, like an artist who took the time to paint every last pixel of every cloud. Colors danced way better than Jamie and I ever did in that high school cafeteria, the sun lighting up the entire sky with one last spectacle before the curtain closed for the day.

In a moment of clarity (more like humility), I realized I wasn't the thing that had caught her eye after all; the sunset had done that. I wasn't the object her camera was focused on; it was pointed at the brilliance on the horizon. She wasn't impressed by me; she was impressed by the beauty behind me.

And then my soulmate packed up her camera and hiked back up the beach before I even made it to shore. She'd never been taking pictures of me. Because she didn't know the plan. She didn't even know I existed. She walked away, unaware that fifty feet behind her there was a guy with a vivid imagination who was now laugh-ing hysterically at himself.

If Bill had been around the beach that day, he probably would've asked me if I was laughing like that as a defense mechanism to shield myself from a deeper wound. But I didn't know Bill at that point, so I just kept laughing.

The Whiteboard

That memory of the photographer that got away swam through my brain as I returned to shore, the humor a welcome distraction from the cold water. After a few minutes of shivering on the beach, I walked back to my car, put on my last "clean" shirt, and headed to the event.

The speaker was a theologian named Tim, whose words struck an uncommon but deeply refreshing balance between brilliance and humility.

Alongside a few other Bible enthusiasts, I walked into the room and sat down as Tim stood up at the whiteboard and did what he did best: launched into three hours of teaching on the kingdom of heaven that brought Jesus's message to life in a whole new way.

The Kingdom of Heaven

Forty days is a long time to stay in the wilderness, especially when you go the entire time without food or water. When Jesus walked back into Capernaum, there was something different about him. Everyone noticed it. Not arrogance, but authority. He spoke less and listened more. But when it was time to talk, people paid attention.

Dozens of followers turned into hundreds. Realizing he had a crowd, he decided to start his first official sermon with a big claim. You get only one chance to make a first impression, and Jesus certainly didn't disappoint: "Repent, for the kingdom of heaven has come near."[1]

The announcement brought the town to a halt. Some were excited. Others were enraged. But no one was left indifferent.

In that small room, Tim explained how Jesus was harking back to the first page of the Bible when God put Adam and Eve on earth to rule over the land. But of course, all of that went horribly wrong. Sin, separation, and death—for thousands of years.

Until this day, when Jesus came on the scene, fresh from the wilderness, and announced that a new reality is now crashing into ours: The kingdom of heaven is at hand—and he is the King of the kingdom.

Jesus was proclaiming that all of Scripture pointed to him. Which is a big statement, unless you can back it up. And that's exactly what he did for the next three and a half years. Every word and action proved his opening words: "Repent, for the kingdom of heaven has come near."

Tim went on to explain how *repent* has become a bit of a cuss-word these days, like Jesus was just being the ultimate killjoy. But understood in the proper context, it's actually a beautiful invitation. *Repent* just means "to change your mind." It means "to stop thinking one way and begin thinking another way." That's what Jesus was doing. He was inviting us to leave our old way of living behind.

"Hey, you know this way you've been living? Turns out, it's not the only way. You've been trying to build your own kingdom. How has that been working out for you? Did you know there is actually another way to live?"

As Tim taught, we were silent, entranced. They say a picture is worth a thousand words, which is probably why I'd given up on words and was now resorting to pictures—scribbling a series of images in my journal.

Imagine there is a throne
at the center of your being.

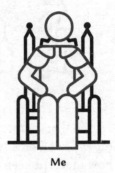

We all have someone on the throne,
a point everything revolves around.
Left to ourselves, we put ourselves
on there and set out to build
our kingdom.

Me

But that's not the only option. As Tim
reminded us, two thousand years ago,
Jesus came on the scene and invited us to
repent, get off the throne, and put Jesus
there. To help build God's kingdom
instead of ours.

Jesus

Easy enough? Here's why
this is so revolutionary
(especially for us single people).
If I'm trying to build my
kingdom, then everything
becomes about how things
either help or hurt me. Every
person and event is about
the kingdom of me.

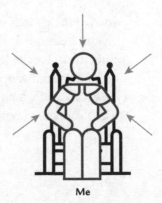

Me

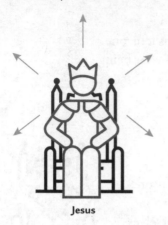

Jesus

However, when things become about a kingdom beyond me, the kingdom of heaven, everything I say and do can become about something bigger than me.

I sat in that room, fresh off a minor freak-out on top of Half Dome twenty-four hours earlier, realizing how much I'd been thinking about myself up there.

God, speak to me.
Give me a revelation.
Show me my next step.
Help me build the kingdom of me.

Even a lot of the fear I was feeling about going to plant a church was rooted in my kingdom. It's not like I was worried the church wouldn't work because of what that would mean for the kingdom of heaven. I was worried because of what it would mean for my own reputation.

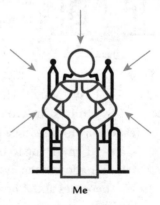

Me

I can't think of a more important lesson for a single person to learn. Because, two thousand years ago, Jesus (who was single, by the way—have I mentioned that yet?) gave us a beautiful invitation out of the madness. He stepped into the middle of the rat race and showed us that something infinitely bigger is going on here.

I felt like a hamster who had been running on a wheel my entire life, expending all the energy with none of the progress. Until the scientist who had been observing me reached down and pulled me off it. Or, more accurately, the scientist became a hamster himself, met me at the wheel, and demonstrated how to step off.

Trade in the kingdom of me for the kingdom of heaven.

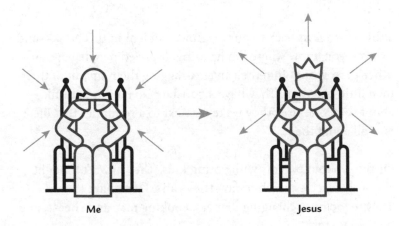

Me   Jesus

Me, Me, Me

There were other people in the room, but Tim was talking right to me. Whether it's watching a girl take pictures on a beach or having a pity party on a mountaintop, I realized how often I make everything about myself.

And now you're thinking, *Well, Ryan, I don't think that's just a you thing. I think every human does that. It's kind of selfish to make selfishness about you.*

See? That's what I'm talking about. I even talk about selfishness selfishly.

It's easy to get stuck in the kingdom of me.

Think about the superstitious fan who can't watch a game without thinking they're affecting it. *Wait a second. They get a first down every time I pet the dog before the snap. Get over here, Ralphie. The team needs me.* No, they don't. You don't matter. You don't change the outcome of the game at all; you just like making things about you.

Which brings us back to our original problem in this book—and by now, you know where I'm heading: Married people have another person built into their lives, dragging them up out of their own little kingdom. They have a constant invitation to think about someone else. They wake up next to a reminder that life isn't all about them.

Or think about parents with young kids. They haven't thought about themselves much today. They can't. Don't have time. They're too busy changing diapers, cooking mac and cheese, and picking up toys.

And if you're a single parent, you haven't thought about yourself in months. You're too busy doing all the aforementioned things but with no backup. Well done. You're excused from the next paragraph. Zone out, or better yet, take a nap.

As a single person, I don't have other people pulling me out of the kingdom of me, so it's easy to let everything become about me. To get stuck in my own little kingdom and let the rest of the world revolve around me. Before I know it, I can't even let someone enjoy a sunset without trying to surf in and make it about me. No one does it on purpose. It's a defect in the design. As God once said, "It is not good for the man to be alone."[2]

Confronting the past and surrendering the future is hard work. It's a lifelong process. But there's still a final piece to the puzzle. You have to work your way out of the kingdom of me by making your life about other people. You have to realize your singleness isn't primarily about you. Once you stir and then still the water, it's time to start sharing it with others.

Remember, singleness is a gift. Gifts are great to receive, but at some point, you realize gifts are a lot more fun to give.

Think about Christmas. When I was a kid, Christmas was all about me. I made a list, counted down the days, and enjoyed every last bit of it. But I'm an adult. Imagine if I were still showing up to my parents' house on Christmas morning, running down the stairs, and pushing my nephew out of the way to get to my pile.

If you watched that happen, you'd have one thought: *Ryan never grew up.*

Because eventually you realize there is a deeper magic to Christmas. As fun as it is to get gifts, it's way better to create that experience for other people.

The magic is in creating Christmas for the next generation.
The magic is in giving Christmas to that family who can't afford it.
The magic is in giving up your Christmas to be with that friend who had a tragic year and is all alone.

At first, life is all about you. And it should be. But if you keep going, keep growing. Keep learning. Eventually, you realize there is a deeper magic. The decision to give your life to that deeper magic, to make your life about other people, is the secret to grounding your life in this present moment.

Want to be content being single today?

Think a lot less about yourself.
And a lot more about others.

Trade in selfish thoughts for selfless ones.

C. S. Lewis aptly said it this way: "Look for yourself, and you will find in the long run only hatred, loneliness, despair, rage, ruin, and decay. But look for Christ and you will find Him, and with Him everything else thrown in."[3]

Per usual, Lewis hit the nail on the head. It's a tough pill to swallow at first, but the day you recognize your propensity to stay stuck in your own little world and decide instead to devote your life to the kingdom of heaven, your life gets infused with the kind of meaning and purpose that make contentment in the present moment possible.

Laying down your own agenda and making life about others feels like a day at the spa for the soul that has been obsessing about itself for years. It's hard to see when you're in it, but as soon as you get a moment of reprieve, it becomes clear as day.

We confront the past. (Stir.)
We surrender the future. (Still.)
And then we wake up every morning and realize our singleness is an amazing gift to give to the world. (Share.)

I wonder if that's one of the reasons Jesus immediately started assembling a group of uneducated and ordinary people to be a part of his movement.[4] He certainly could've moved a lot faster on his own, but community has always been the point (more on that in chapter 11).

The rest of this book is about the daily practice of getting off the throne—trading in the kingdom of me for the kingdom of heaven.

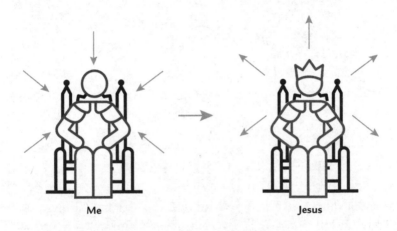

Me   Jesus

The kingdom of heaven is at hand. It's an invitation to step off the throne and concede that spot to Jesus by trying to live like him—a generous, simple life that looks less like making your name great and more like empowering others. That looks less like trying to be first and more like serving people. That looks less like holding grudges and more like going to great lengths to forgive everyone.

After the conference, I drove down the coast for what would be the last time for several years, now with a brand-new outlook on life—a goal to stop making my life about my own little kingdom.

I just didn't know how hard it would be to pull it off.

These final chapters are about the very beginning of my journey of trying to step out of the kingdom of me. I continue to get it wrong all the time and don't know much. But I have learned one thing along the way: Being a kid at Christmas is fun, but being an adult can be truly magical—it's just a bit of an acquired taste.

Chapter 10

Conflict, Connection, and Contentment

Discover the Benefits of True Community

"Do you want to preach in the relationship series?"

My brother's question caught me off guard. We were sitting on a patio in the middle of February (because you can do stuff like that in Austin, Texas). It was my twenty-ninth birthday, and we were eating sushi.

Our church was six weeks old at the time, and we felt how I imagine parents feel when their first kid is six weeks old. Tired, unqualified, and trying not to think about the fact that we had to keep this going every week from here on out.

After my pilgrimage to Yosemite and a pit stop in Denver for some planning, we moved to Austin. When I say "we," I mean Doug and his wife (Sam), Ethan and his wife (Stef), and about thirty other amazing people from Colorado and California who were willing to take a crazy step and be part of the journey. Getting there and figuring out how to get the church started is another story for another day, but on January 6, 2019, we launched Red Rocks Austin.

Six weeks later, we were heading into a relationship series, and I was trying to ignore the elephant in the room. An elephant my brother had just woken up between bites of sashimi.

"I, uh . . ." I said with the opposite of confidence. "I don't know, man."

We laughed. I didn't need to explain myself any further.

"You could always talk about singleness," he suggested.

"No one wants to listen to that," I told him immediately, putting down my miso soup as all my insecurities came back to the surface. You can't really plant a church with two married guys and avoid people pointing out what makes you different. Everyone knew I was single, and the usual jokes were flying around, but something about spending the whole weekend focused on it made me cringe. "Plus, this isn't a young-adult service anymore," I told him. "It's 'big church.' What are all the married people going to do for thirty-five minutes?"

"At some point," he said calmly, "you should just embrace your singleness." Those words sparked something in the depths of my soul. Something that was more like a match being struck in the middle of a rainy night—quickly extinguished. Meanwhile, my brother just picked up a piece of salmon and shrugged.

I told him I'd come up with something generic that everyone could relate to. But even that thought was making me anxious. *Is there something wrong with me?*

After dinner, we passed a clothing store on our way to a friend's apartment. The mannequin in the window caught my eye. It was wearing a shiny black-and-gold bomber jacket. "I should preach my relationship sermon in that," I told Doug.

"Really? It's not really you," he said. (It wasn't.)

"Maybe it'll be my new style," I told him. (It wouldn't.)

Quick story: When I was in high school, I played football. Friday was game night, but then we'd gather in the film room on Saturday morning to watch every play from the night before. My coach would keep hitting pause mid-play and break it down. He'd zoom in on the route I was running and ask me questions about what was going through my head. It was helpful—painful but helpful.

Let's do the same thing for this story. Hit the pause button, zoom in, and dissect it.

I was with my brother, the person I trust most in this world, enjoying sushi on my birthday. He brought up the topic I hoped would come up, the one I needed a safe space to talk through. As you know by now, singleness had always created uneasiness in my soul and, as a result, produced conflict between me and anyone who joked or even asked a sincere question about it. There I was, with a golden opportunity to embrace the conflict and learn from it, but instead, I punted on the opportunity.

If my football coach had been watching this story with me (and suddenly transformed from a football fanatic to a caring counselor), he would've asked what was going through my head at that moment. I would've told him I spent most of my life running away from conflict and calling it noble.

Then he would've hit play on the scene, and we would've witnessed something called retail therapy. Because instead of taking time to sit with the discomfort, emotions, and insecurities I was feeling, I marched past the mannequin and bought the jacket.

And never wore it.

Cookie-Cutter
A few weeks later, I preached the sermon. It was fine. And fine is the right word. People told me it was great, but people always say

that. I took the church through Psalm 23 (that famous one about the Lord being our shepherd), and I called it "A Song for Every Situation." This was my crafty way of saying, without realizing it at the time, that whether you're single, dating, engaged, or married, you can be content.

Like I said, people said it was great.

But I drove home feeling like a phony.

I had an opportunity to embrace the conflict in my own soul, to dive into the depths and ask myself why I stay single and whether or not that's really what I want and all that. But I passed on the opportunity and covered it up with a generic sermon.

I had an opportunity to craft a custom sermon. Instead, I went cookie-cutter.

And again, if my football coach had hit pause mid-sermon and asked me why I chose to do that, I would've shrugged and mumbled, "Custom costs more." Crafting something custom means coming face-to-face with the monsters under the bed, the skeletons in the closet. Creating custom art requires a willingness to embrace the conflict within. To fight and ask yourself what you really believe. It's a beautifully brutal process, but I wasn't ready to dive headfirst into the conflicted feelings I was having about my singleness.

Instead, I ran.

The Gift of Conflict

A few months later, I had lunch with my friend Chad. Chad is a communicator extraordinaire who seems to always believe the stuff he's talking about. I bet he wouldn't preach "A Song for Every Situation." He'd probably get alone and sit and pray and all that spiritual stuff until he was ready to craft something that cost him. Something that would make the rest of us cry.

He's also good at asking questions. The real ones. The ones that lead to great conversations. Like a master painter, he uses questions to turn an ordinary lunch into an extraordinary experience—Picasso with words.

We sat down to have lunch at a hidden gem called Valencia's. A Tex-Mex spot hidden in plain sight, right in the middle of one of the busiest parts of Austin.

I figured my new bomber jacket would be overkill for Tex-Mex, so I wore a T-shirt. Chad and I sat down and started taking down a basket of chips and salsa, both talking a big game about our new diets, how much better we felt, and how we were going to take it easy because we were heading to the gym later. "Queso? We probably should. Guac too. And tacos."

Neither of us made it to the gym.

However, I did walk out of the restaurant with a realization that has been haunting me in the best way ever since. Chad was doing what he did best. Casually pressing in with questions. He was single for several years longer than he wanted to be before he met his wife, so he knows what to ask.

"If I'm being honest," I said about thirty minutes into the conversation, "I am great at searching for and finding red flags."

He didn't look up from his taco. He just asked me why I thought that was.

"Because, most of the time, I don't really want to be in a relationship and so red flags are my friends—they reaffirm my narrative and reaffirm my own rightness."

He encouraged me and reminded me he'd be just as happy about me staying single the rest of my life. But then he dropped the line I can't stop thinking about.

"One thing I'll say," he said with a smile and all the grace in the world. "That part about being quick to find red flags—that's not why Jesus was single."

Have you ever had a moment that felt like someone turned on the lights in a dark room? That last line descended into the basement of my soul and flipped on a switch that had been collecting dust for decades.

It wouldn't have taken a professional like Bill to notice that pushing people away had become a habit in my life.

She's too serious.
She's too silly.
She's too quiet.
She's too talkative.

Identifying red flags is an essential part of dating. But this isn't a book about dating, and those aren't red flags. They're eject buttons. Cheap escape pods.

As Chad talked, my mind raced. He was right. Keeping people at a distance is a specialty of mine. It's a convenient way to avoid conflict.

If you aren't that close with someone, it's not a big deal if they walk away.
If you aren't that close with someone, disagreements can just be swept under the rug.
If you aren't that close with anyone, you can live a life free from drama.

You can course correct and avoid conflict. But the cost is steep. Because healthy conflict is actually a gift; it's an opportunity for greater connection. And that connection is the secret to being and staying present in the moment—to being single today.

Before we go any further, note I said "*healthy* conflict." When I use the word *conflict* in this chapter, I'm referring to conflict based on mutual respect and trust, where the goal is trying to get better together rather than win an argument.

Jesus wasn't afraid of conflict. And if my goal is to try to live like him, I can't just say, "See, Jesus was single, so I'll be single too," as an excuse to push people away. Yes, Jesus was single, but he also had deep, authentic friendships. He had lifelong friends he ferociously loved.

There's a reason Jesus was single, but it wasn't because he wanted to dodge true connection. And it certainly wasn't because he wanted to run away from conflict. So why was Jesus single? This would have to turn into a thick theology book to attempt to give any sort of definitive answer, and I'm probably not the person for the job. So here's one answer that aligns more with the style of the rest of these chapters: Maybe Jesus was single to show each person (regardless of relational status) what it looks like to live with a heart wide open to everyone. And maybe that's one of the reasons he was so good at being present in the moment.

When a heart is closed, every imperfection is a red flag. But when a heart is open, imperfections are invitations to closer relationship. They bring us together. They draw us deeper. They are solicitations for grace.

This is why some of your closest friendships on this planet are with people you've been through hell with.

The conflict is rarely fun, but the connection on the other side is worth it. At least, that's my hypothesis—and has been ever since Chad's question turned that light on in my soul.

I'm writing this chapter at the risk of you thinking I've got this down. (*None of us are thinking that, Ryan.*) I don't. (*Really? We're all shocked.*) I'm working on it, slowly figuring out how to open my heart to the world. It's just that I've noticed a pattern: The people I know who are truly content and present today have a lot of deep connections in their lives—connections they've had to fight through conflict to build.

So, if I had to summarize this section, it'd go something like this:

> We all want connection.
> Healthy conflict is necessary to have deep connection.
> Contentment comes when we put the necessary effort into conflict and our connection deepens.

Because when you're single, it's important to stir and still the water, but ultimately you have to share it. Our existence is about developing deep, genuine friendships with people where they have a chance to be imperfect. Where mistakes are opportunities for grace and growth. Where conflict is a gift that leads to greater connection. Where singleness stops being an excuse to avoid conflict and becomes an opportunity to live like Jesus.

Conflict: An Entry Point

Here's an important question every single person should wrestle with: Why do we get so frustrated when people bring up our singleness?

It usually takes a lot to make me angry, but back then, around that lunch I had with Chad, I'd get combative as soon as someone asked me a question about my love life.

Every relative checking in during a holiday meal.
Every friend calling to catch up.
Every stranger trying to start some semblance of small talk.

I'd start shaking, perceiving a genuine question from a good
friend or family member to be an all-out assault on my lifestyle.

Why?

The answer, at least for me, comes down to two words: *perception*
and *reflection.*

It took me a long time to realize my *perception* of the external
world is often a *reflection* of my internal reality. Said more practically, I didn't like talking about singleness because I was afraid to
confront it internally.

It was easier to feel combative toward the questioner than it was
to enter into my own questions. I'd go to war against the person
across the table a thousand times over before I'd look in the mirror. *Inner conflict? No thanks. I'll just push those feelings back
down and buy another jacket.*

But that's not why Jesus was single. You can't fast for forty days
alone in the wilderness if you're afraid of your inner world. He
was well acquainted with the water in his soul—at peace with
himself.

Because of the peace Jesus had in his inner world, conflict in the
outer world was nothing more than another opportunity for
deeper connection.

Now, back to our question. Why get so combative when people
ask you about your singleness? Obviously, some people in your
life really will be stirring up unhealthy conflict. And you should
have boundaries and all that. But if you always feel like the people

who love you are being antagonistic when they bring up your singleness, it may be because there is a war in your soul. Your perception of what they're asking may be a reflection of what's going on in you.

Or at least that's what happens to me. So, taking a cue from my high school football coach, when conflict comes, I'm learning to hit pause and evaluate what's happening in my soul. Because inner conflict isn't something to run away from; it's a door to walk through. It's an entry point into deeper connection.

When I feel the frustration coming on, I tell myself, *Stop getting mad; start getting curious.*

In the process, I've started finding answers to all the real questions, the ones you've probably been asking the whole time you've been reading this book.

Why did I panic during that dance with Jamie?
Why did that Instagram post from that ex send me for such a loop?
Why did I freak out during that wedding?
Why do all my defense mechanisms spring into action at the mention of romantic love?

And most importantly, *Why has this been a pattern all these years?*

Here's the answer: *I kept running away from the conflict instead of through it.* You can't heal from something you don't have the courage to sit with. I was in the habit of running, so I was missing out on opportunities for deep connection and contentment.

I didn't find any answers about why I was sitting in church parking lots at night until I sat down with Bill and let him ask me questions. When I did, I realized I actually had a lot of unprocessed shame from the past. Shame that I figured I was stuck with, until I started talking about it. It was the inner conflict that set me free.

I didn't find any semblance of peace until I stopped skirting around conversations with my friends and family about the future. When I did, I learned I carried a deep fear of the future around with me everywhere I went. The shot clock was real for me—the tomorrow trap had me in its clutches. And it was the difficult conversations, the confrontation, the conflict, that set me free.

How about you? Is there any conflict you've been avoiding? I wonder if that conflict would lead to deeper connection and contentment if you could find the courage to step into it.

Because again . . .

> Connection is the deep desire of our souls.
> Conflict is a doorway into deeper connection.
> Contentment is the fruit that follows.

Some Super Official Research to Back Up My Claim

I know I'm making some pretty big statements in this chapter about connection being the deepest craving of your soul and all that. But since you can't really just say that without backing it up, here is my super official data to prove my claim. I mean, this is the stuff. The "use this in your senior thesis" research:

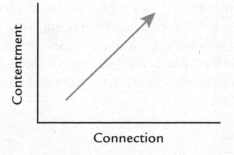

What do you think? Pretty profound, right? You're welcome.

We are created for connection. Connection with our Creator and with other people. The more genuine connection we get with people, the more contentment we feel—which is why you drive home from a dinner with great friends feeling like you're on cloud nine.

It's also why when you spend a whole day working from home in a job that doesn't have any human contact, you start to feel like something is off. The pandemic in 2020 was a giant case study of the effect of disconnection. You can chart the results on a graph:

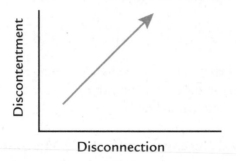

(*Wait a second. Isn't that the same graph? He just flipped the words.*)

And that's not just true about connecting with our Creator and other people either; it's also true about connecting with creation. I was talking to my ninety-three-year-old grandpa last Christmas. My grandma was making BLTs, so he was heading out to the garden in his backyard to pick the final tomato of the season. He went on to explain that they usually don't stay ripe this long, but since it had been a warm fall in California, the last tomato made it all the way to Christmas.

I was smiling as he talked, because he's ninety-three and still tends a garden. Sure, he could go buy tomatoes, but he's working on his tenth decade of life, and along the way, he's discovered how good it is for us to stay connected with the Creator, with creation, and with one another.

He's connected.
And he's content.

I can't even tell you when tomatoes are in season. Or how to know if they're ripe. I'm not saying we all need to drop what we're doing and start a garden, but it's fair to point out that the more disconnected we get from creation, the more stressed out and empty we seem to feel.

Maybe that's why people in beach towns tend to be laid back and happy but people in cities tend to be frustrated and uptight. The former have a place where they can reconnect with creation on their lunch break. The latter have it as their screen saver.

When disconnection goes up, contentment goes down. Here's what I mean:

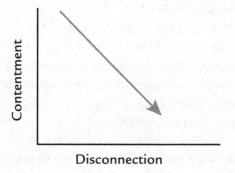

(Wait. Now he thinks he's making a brand-new point with the wordplay?)

We're becoming more and more disconnected, and in the process, we seem to be losing our ability to stay present and content.

I know this is a really research-heavy chapter, but stick with me, because I promise we're going somewhere. Now that we've examined the relationship between contentment and disconnection, we're ready to put all the pieces together and discuss the relationship between discontentment and connection.

It looks like this:

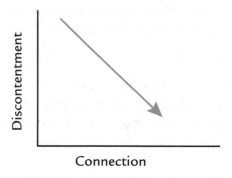

(I don't think I like this chapter.)

Beyond the Kingdom of Me

I laughed way too hard writing that last section. And I don't mean to keep circling the boat, but we have to get this. You can form deep connections with God, creation, and people while you're single, but you have to get intentional about embracing the healthy conflict that helps you climb out of the trap of thinking life is only about your own little kingdom.

Again, emphasis on the word *healthy*. I know there's an unhealthy version of conflict. Some people love to search for drama. Not to get out of their own little kingdom, but to justify staying in it. That's not the type of conflict I'm talking about.

When I was eating sushi with my brother, he was inviting me into *healthy conflict.* He was like a herald riding into my kingdom with a message that there was more beyond the walls of my little castle. But of course, there would be battles to fight out there too—conflict and confrontation. His question about preaching in the relationship series was an invitation to embrace the conflict and experience the connection and contentment on the other side. Outside the confines of the kingdom of me.

The questions that make you insecure or uneasy about your own singleness are a gift. They're an opportunity to confront the conflict. Or you can just push it down, run into a store, and buy a jacket.

That's usually how it goes, isn't it?

Just as the rough water is about to still long enough for us to see clearly, just when we begin to notice the narrative that's been lulling us to sleep—keeping us thinking about ourselves, allowing us to be the king or queen of our own little lonely kingdom—just when our eyes are about to open and see outside our own world for a moment so we can connect with others, we panic and look for a way to numb the pain.

But today you have another opportunity to say yes to the conflict. Maybe it means showing some tough love to a friend who needs someone to be honest with them about the path they're on. Maybe it means being honest with that family member about why you're so upset with them. Maybe it means apologizing for the thing causing a rift between you and your ex. Maybe it means talking to a counselor about an unhealthy relational pattern you see in yourself. That conflict looks different for everyone, but the invitation is the same—confront it and experience the real connection and contentment on the other side. Decide to make life about truly connecting with others. And then make that decision over and over again.

Every hour.
Every minute.
Every breath.

I'll end this chapter by transcribing my thought process whenever I decide to actually say yes. To think about what I'm thinking about and start asking questions of the question-asker. To embrace the conflict in my own mind, reconnect with myself, and enjoy the contentment that follows.

Is there something wrong with me?
Am I getting this whole thing wrong?
Wait. Getting what wrong?
Wrong according to who?
Why do I spend so much time in my own head?
Why do I make this whole thing about me?
Look around. There's a bigger and more beautiful story unfolding all around me.
Who cares about my own silly little reputation?
I'm not the entire puzzle. I'm a piece, playing my part the best I can.
There isn't something wrong with me. I just need to get out of my own head and see the bigger picture.
Take a breath, Ryan. Relax. And be single today.

Chapter 11

Single, Not Alone

Experience the Gift of Good Friends

On February 29, 2020, John Mulaney hosted *Saturday Night Live.*

I remember that day well because it was the night before our first church service in a new building we were renting. Our church was fifteen months old at the time, and my bomber jacket had been collecting dust in my closet for just over a year.

We were at the building until late that night, making sure every-thing was ready to go. When I got home, I was exhausted and nervous and ready to take my mind off the church.

John Mulaney is one of my favorite comedians, so when I saw that his opening monologue was already on YouTube, I made some Sleepytime tea and sat down to watch. The whole mono-logue was great, but in the middle of it, he said one of the more profound things I'd heard in a while:

> It is hard to make friends when you're an adult male.
> I think that the greatest miracle of Jesus, truly, is that he was
> a thirty-three-year-old man and he had twelve best friends.
> And they were not his wife's friends' husbands.[1]

I was that guy laughing audibly on my couch by myself when I heard that, because it's true. The older you get, the harder it be-comes to have authentic friendships.

When you're young, friendship is available naturally. You get to school, and everyone else is looking for friends, so you find your people. Your thing. Maybe it's sports. Or plays. Or band. Whatever you're into, there are bound to be some other people around who are into the same thing. In college, there are dorms, Greek life, majors, clubs, hangouts, and parties.

But then, after college, people go their separate ways, and finding a solid community isn't quite as easy. And as friends get married, you see them less and less. Five times a week becomes three times a week, then maybe one if you're lucky.

It's not a matter of *if*. It's a matter of *when*. It's just reality. Things change. Life happens. People keep growing. And it's a beautiful thing, but it also presents a challenge.

When your friends start getting married, suddenly they have the person they confide in. Someone in their corner, their best friend. And it isn't you. So you look for another. But then they get married. And so on and so forth.

I think that's why I laughed so hard at Mulaney's joke. I felt it at a visceral level.

As we get older, we grow apart from people, but we never outgrow our need for the connection we talked about in the last chapter.

It's like staying in shape. The older you get, the more challenging it becomes. It's easy to give up on it, but if you want to be single like Jesus, you don't get to give up; you need to double down and get serious about finding your people.

It's in the Details

If you paid close attention to the date in the story above, the answer is yes. We opened a brand-new church location two weeks before the world shut down for COVID. Those first two weekends were special, but then the world went on lockdown, and we figured we were done for.

Around that time, my buddy Zach started a car detailing business. I didn't know what that meant, but I was proud of him for being proactive during the pandemic, so I hired him to detail my car and figured he was just going to come over for thirty minutes and wash it, maybe vacuum out the inside if he had time. When he texted me to tell me he was on his way, I threw away the trash in my back seat, brought in the bomber jacket I'd left in my trunk, and figured the car was ready.

Zach didn't just show up; he rolled up in a personalized van with a whole bunch of special gismos and gadgets. For the next four hours, he worked diligently, detailing every square inch of my car.

When he was done, it felt like an entirely different car. I was blown away and just kept thanking him over and over again.

"Yeah, no problem," he said as he left to head to his next appointment. "Oh, by the way, I put all your stuff in a bag over there."

"Oh, you mean like my jumper cables?" I asked.

"Yeah," he said, smiling. "Like your jumper cables." Then he got in his van and drove off. When I walked over to the bag of stuff, I started laughing (mostly out of embarrassment). It wasn't just my jumper cables. It was a massive bag full of the most random items. Here are a few of the highlights:

- a Peyton Manning rookie card
- a single Keurig pod
- a Panera gift card with $1.23 left
- some anointing oil
- an NSYNC CD

If you'd gotten in my car before Zach came over, you might've thought it was clean, but you would've been wrong. My car wasn't clean. I just figured out a way to make it look that way. You saw the good part; all the trash was hidden in secret compartments.

The world saw my best, and I hid the rest.

I'm not sure if I was fooling people, but I was certainly fooling myself. Until Zach showed up in his van and spent four hours cleaning out the rest and putting it in a bag. That bag, I realized, was a reminder of three questions every single person should be asking.

Do I have people in my life who are detailing my car?
Have I given people permission to look at my blind spots?
Will I actually listen to them when they point them out?

If the answer is no, there is a strong chance your car isn't nearly as clean as you think it is. Which means you probably aren't as fully known as you think you are.

Married people have an accountability system built in. They have someone who is constantly detailing their car. Someone who is calling them on their bad habits and pointing out their blind spots. Singles don't. We have to go find it. We may be single, but we aren't called to be alone. And if you want to be fully loved by others, you have to allow yourself to be fully known.

Fully Known and Fully Loved
My first year of college was one of the most pivotal years of my life. When I moved to Boulder, I wasn't sure if I was Christian, atheist, or agnostic. You know you're on a journey when you can't even commit to being agnostic.

By the end of my freshman year, I was obsessed with all the Jesus stories in the Bible. I devoured every last bit of content I could get my hands on. The love, grace, truth, and subversive strategy of Jesus were contagious—I was hooked. Several ingredients went into the transformation I experienced my freshman year, but one of the biggest was two senior guys who started a small group and invited me to join. When you're eighteen, a couple of twenty-two-year-olds seem like the coolest people in the world, so I said yes.

One of the seniors was a guy from Pittsburgh named Brandon, and the other was a guy from Laguna Beach named Sam (whose mom, Sally, would later say, "I don't care. I don't care. I think that means she cares"). They also invited two other guys to the group—Doug and our friend Ethan, who keep coming up in this book because of their influence on my life.

Doug, Ethan, and I drove to the first meeting together and had no idea what to expect. Honestly, I didn't even know what a small group was. None of us had ever done anything like this before, and as we drove, we were hesitant. We even made a pact that no matter what these weird Christians said to us, we would never stop doing what we did best: throwing parties.

I bet that was one of those moments that made God smile. Because the truth is, we stayed true to our word. We have never stopped throwing parties; it's just that our parties look a little different these days. They still involve lots of loud music and laughter, but they happen on Sunday instead of Friday, and people leave feeling inspired, motivated, and loved instead of intoxicated.

But that's a story for another day.

We walked into the small group having no idea what to expect and walked out a few hours later with a deep sense that whatever had just happened, we needed more of it in our lives. For the next four years, we met every Thursday night. We'd read books or study Scripture together, but the thing that really shifted things around in our souls was that we'd go around the circle and take a few minutes to check in. We'd tell everyone how our week was. We'd talk about the things we were struggling with, and we'd celebrate the things that were going well.

And for three college kids who spent most of their time just thinking about how to have a good time, it was a completely new experience.

That changed everything.

We were from different walks of life, but the connections came easily. The check-ins were pretty safe and simple at first, but we slowly realized we could be honest about the real things we were struggling with, and instead of being isolated like we feared, we'd stand side by side and fight for freedom together.

Because I wanted to be loved, I was terrified to be fully known. But letting people into those places and realizing I was still loved was the secret sauce to transformation. The more we experienced those true soul-level connections, the less appealing all the counterfeit connections became. The cheap knockoff versions lost their appeal.

Is There Something Wrong with Me?
After college, we decided the group was too good to let go of. So, for well over a decade now, we've been getting together once a year to check in and talk about what is going on in our lives.

A few years ago, we went to Hilton Head. We rode bikes, ate good food, played a lot of bocce ball, and had a blast.

But the part I'll never forget was my check-in. My turn came around on the last day when we were down on the beach. No matter how many times I've done something like that, it's a little scary. Vulnerability always is. I could feel the watchful soldiers who try to protect the deep parts of my soul stand to attention.

But the beautiful thing about having such a close connection with these guys is that they knew exactly what I was feeling, so they smiled, nodded, and encouraged me to share everything.

They are all married with kids.

Their struggles are all very different from mine.

I know nothing about the demons they face. But they don't know about the demons single people have to face. Regardless, they showed up and were ready to go there with me.

I began to tell them about how scared I'd been to talk about singleness. How uncomfortable of a subject it's been for me historically. And as they asked me why, I blurted out, "Because I've always felt like there is something wrong with me."

And that's when the waterworks began.

I started telling them about the feeling you get when you realize that all your friends have a deep desire for something that appears to be missing in your heart. Like there is something off about you. I told them how people always ask me questions that make me feel like I'm missing something. Like I've screwed something up. Like I'm the only one who isn't in on some big inside joke.

And although I wasn't saying anything I hadn't already realized, I was speaking it out loud, surrounded by real humans who I had real connections with. And that made all the difference. That's where the waterworks were coming from. My tears were water I was sharing with my friends.

My best friends didn't think there was something wrong with me. They weren't secretly waiting for me to get married to let me back into the group. They just love me because of who I am. Single and all.

And as you read that, you may be thinking, *Well, yeah. Duh.*

I'd say the same thing if I were hearing about your experience. It's easy for me to believe that kind of love is true for others, but it's difficult for me to believe it's true for me.

But when it sank in that it really is true for me, it changed everything.
The freedom I felt.
The love I felt.
The acceptance I felt.

Is there something wrong with me? No. I mean, yeah, probably lots of things. But no, because being different doesn't disqualify me from the really deep friendships in life. And at the end of the day, connection is all that really matters. Besides, what does that question even mean? It presupposes that there is a right way for me to be. As if all of life is an exam that I'm failing. And my wrong answers disqualify me from community and render me unfit to be with people.

As I spoke, my friends sat on a beach and debunked that entire narrative. Maybe life is less about right and wrong and more about being together.

Tim Keller once said, "To be loved but not known is comforting but superficial. To be known and not loved is our greatest fear. But to be fully known and truly loved is, well, a lot like being loved by God."[2] That's the gift I was given in Hilton Head. A deep, genuine connection. Because deep connection isn't reserved for married folks. It looks different in friendships, but the heart-level vulnerability and love are available for any group of friends who are willing to put in the work to get there. Who are willing to dive down past the shallow waters of small talk and discuss the things really going on.

You may be single, but you aren't alone.

The four Gospels are the highlight reel of Jesus's life. But think about how much is left out. We wouldn't be able to contain the endless stories of Jesus and his friends' experiences. John, one of his best friends, tells us as much.[3]

We get the ministry moments, but what about the friendship moments? The jokes flying around the dinner table while they ate some good food. The stories told as they walked from one town to the next. The late-night questions about life's deepest mysteries around the fire. The honest conversations about fears and insecurities as they camped under the stars. And the magically mundane moments as they went through everyday life.

Jesus developed deep, lifelong friendships with people. The type that would later convince them to give up their lives, to trade in everything to continue his mission and carry his message of love to the ends of the earth. Mulaney called those deep friendships a miracle. I call them the fruit of vulnerability and consistency.

Lots of times when I tell people that story about Hilton Head, they respond, "Well, that's great for you, Ryan. But I don't have a group of friends I've been meeting with for a decade."

I get it. Loneliness is real, and although there are things you can do to increase your odds of finding community, at some level it feels like playing the lottery. Sometimes it just doesn't work out. But I'd say it's more like a job. If you keep showing up, keep doing the work, keep being the type of friend you would want someone else to be for you, you will find your people.

I was talking to my friend Shannon the other day. Remember, she's my therapist friend who has all the same married friends that I do. The one who taught me about the importance of grieving all the way back in chapter 2. We were talking about how lucky we are that our married friends bring us into everything and don't make it weird.

"What do you tell other single people who feel like they are cast out of their social circle once their friends get married?" I asked her.

Like I said in chapter 2, her day job is to work with people who are steeped in drug addiction, so she doesn't hold back. "I mean, if your people base your value on your relationship status, you don't need a relationship to fix that. You need new people."

That was one of those statements that was so true, the only thing I could do was laugh. She's right. If your community of friends need you to fit a certain mold (get married) to still value you as a person, then it's probably time to find some new friends.

The good news is, there are lots of people out there for you. There really are. The bad news is, they aren't just going to show up, knock on your door, and hand you their résumé to be your best friend. Finding community is no different from any other worthwhile endeavor; it takes work.

How did Jesus find friends? By walking down the beach and asking a few fishermen if they wanted to hang out. And when things got challenging or they said things he didn't like, he didn't run away from the conflict; he ran through it.

Jesus showed us the way. He may have been single, but he wasn't alone. He taught us how to embrace conflict and find the gift of connection and contentment that comes from deep community.

But there's more. He also came to remind us that he knows how it feels to be human.

Which is invaluable for single people.

Because, at the end of the day, Jesus knows how you feel.

That loneliness you felt last night—Jesus knows how that feels.
That pain you felt because of the rejection—Jesus knows how that feels.
That betrayal you experienced from that friend group—Jesus knows how that feels.

The truth is, you're not alone. You're never alone.

In my lesser moments, that feels like cold comfort. But it's not. It's true. And according to Scripture, there is a day when we'll all gather together.[4] I don't know how it works on the other side of eternity, but it seems like worship and community will be at the center of whatever we're doing. We'll be together, except without all the competition, lying, envy, and selfish ambition.

That's a vision I can get behind. Knowing that about tomorrow makes it easier to get out of bed and build community for others today.

There are a lot of other single people who feel alone. You have an opportunity to step in and help them see that's not true. You have an opportunity today to break down the social walls we put up around our souls. To ask someone how they're really doing. To sit with them in their pain. To let them know they may be suffering but they don't have to suffer by themselves.

Because they may be single but they aren't alone.

Chapter 12

Flip the Script on Singleness

Stop Waiting for Permission

I love coffee shops. The smell. The atmosphere. The caffeine. Being surrounded by other people who are creating and knowing you can talk to them if you want but don't have to if you don't. Coffee shops are my happy place.

One fateful afternoon in January 2021, I was sitting in one of my favorite shops, when I got a FaceTime from Doug and Ethan. I have enough self-awareness to know I talk too loudly when I'm on a call, so I stepped outside.

"Let's get the teaching schedule locked in for the relationship series really quick," Doug said to us. That request may sound familiar to you. For the record, we don't do a relationship series every other month or anything. This was two years after that sushi dinner we had on my twenty-ninth birthday.

Doug and Ethan started kicking around their ideas for sermons, mostly about marriage and the importance of communicating with your spouse and yada yada.

"What if I kicked the series off," I said, interrupting their banter, "with a sermon on singleness?"

"Yeah?" they both said in surprised unison.

"Yeah," I said. "Then you guys take the rest of the series."

That's all it took. With ten simple words, I walked off the plank and dove into the subject I swore I'd never touch. I took a deep breath and a sip of my Americano; then the floodgates opened alongside my new Word document.

Playing Offense

Remember how I told you about high school football? How we'd sit down Saturday morning and break down the film from the night before? During one film session my senior year, I learned a lesson I've been trying to apply to my life ever since.

I was a wide receiver (the one who stays to the outside and catches passes, relying more on speed than strength). But my final year, my coach wanted me to play defense as well—cornerback (the one who tries to shut the receivers down).

Playing both sides means never coming out of the game. In practice, I wore it like a badge of honor. But when the first game rolled around, I quickly realized it was a bad idea. We got the ball first, drove down, and scored. I caught a few passes and was feeling confident. But then it was time to play defense, and my legs locked up.

The thing about playing cornerback is you're out on an island. You're the last line of defense. If the running back or receiver gets past you, they have a free path to the end zone.

Some people thrive off that energy—I hate it.

Our opponents ran the ball on first down. Then on second, I got beat deep, and they scored a quick touchdown.

In the film room the next morning, I felt like I was watching two different players.

Offense: Confident and ready.
Defense: Scared and unsure.

After the third game of the season, I walked into my coach's office like Ryan Gosling from *Remember the Titans* and said, "Put Petey in. He's better."[1]

My coach looked at me with gratitude, like I'd spared him the difficult conversation coming later that afternoon. He pulled me off defense and let me focus all my attention on what I was good at: offense.

When I played offense, I was playing to win. When I played defense, I was playing not to lose. And there's a big difference. A difference that expands much further than football.

When you're sitting on the throne, you have a lot to guard, like an entire kingdom. You spend your life looking behind you, seeing nothing but possessions to protect—you play defense.

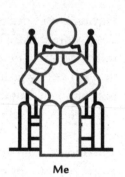

Me

You use your words to put up a wall and reinforce your reputation.

You use your strength to dig a moat and safeguard your status.

You place people in two categories: protectors or threats. You keep the ones helping you protect your kingdom close until you sense they may become a threat. Once that happens, they stop being a human to love and become an enemy to avoid.

No time for offense, you have a kingdom to protect. You aren't playing to win. You are playing not to lose.

Jesus lived the opposite way. He welcomed everyone, always. He didn't bother playing defense; he was too busy playing offense. Then he gave us an invitation to live the same way.

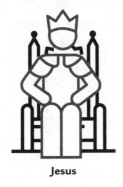

Jesus

When Jesus is on the throne, you stop worrying about protecting your little kingdom and start playing offense. You stop looking behind and start looking ahead.

Words become tools to build people up. Actions become occasions to love. Today becomes one giant opportunity to encourage and inspire.

Jesus once said he would build his church so that "the gates of hell shall not prevail against it."[2] I've always loved that he said "gates." He didn't say, "Hell won't be able to invade our four church walls." That would be a defensive mindset. Jesus invites us to play offense and take the attack forward, to the very gates of hell.

That day in the coffee shop, I figured it was time to take a cue from my seventeen-year-old self. I realized I didn't want to spend my life playing defense, avoiding the topic of singleness because it was a threat to my own little kingdom.

So I told Doug and Ethan I was ready to preach on it.
I was ready to flip it.
To start playing offense.
By helping others do the same.

Which brings us back to that narrative, that script I inherited as a young pastor. The one about how I'm single so I must be looking to mingle. How being single past a certain point meant there must be something wrong. Never mind that we're singing songs about a man who was celibate while we meditate on letters written by a man who was single—marriage is a must. Remember that script? The one creating dissonance in my soul, leaving me sitting in church parking lots, complaining to my spiritual director, having panic attacks during weddings, searching for answers on top of Half Dome, overreacting during birthday dinners, and buying bomber jackets.

I was stuck because I was asking the wrong question.

Defense: Is there something wrong with me?
Offense: What opportunities do my current life circumstances open up for me today?

As I sat in the coffee shop, typing ferociously, I realized what I wanted to say in my first-ever sermon on singleness. That Jesus gave you, me, and everyone else who has ever lived a giant green light to flip the script. To trade in defense for offense. To stop stressing about what yesterday and tomorrow mean for our own little kingdom and start focusing on building God's kingdom today.

Because once you stir and still the water, you realize life is actually about sharing it!

Permission Pending/Permission Granted
In elementary school, I needed a hall pass to leave the room. If I wanted to use the restroom, I had to raise my hand, ask permission (using "may I" instead of "can I" to avoid the grammar lesson), and then carry around a giant stick that said "Mrs. Coke's class." I get why elementary schools do that, but I also remember a day, decades later, when I realized I still carried that hard-wiring.

When I moved to Austin, I bought a townhome. It was my first time purchasing a home, and on day one, I was ecstatic. Then on day two, I was overwhelmed.

What do I do?
What furniture should I buy?
How do I decorate?
Don't I need a theme or something?

All the questions were paralyzing. It took me a few days to realize the answer: I can do whatever I want; every square inch is mine. I don't need a hall pass. I don't need to run my plan by Chip and Joanna Gaines. Permission isn't pending; permission is granted.

That's one of the scripts single people need to flip. Humans, in general, don't like making decisions. I don't think I need to prove my point, but I will. Have you ever been in a car full of adults trying to figure out where to go for lunch? There you go. Point made. Case closed. Making decisions is tough because if it goes wrong, the person who made the choice feels the burden of the blame, so you read twenty Yelp reviews before deciding to go to the same old place you always go.

In a healthy relationship, the two lovebirds shoulder that burden together.

When you're single, you have to hold it up on your own, and the weight can be crushing. The single person who doesn't want the burden ends up waiting for permission to live.

Decorating your home is one thing, but what about that single friend who has been talking about moving to that city for the past five years? Or bringing up the same business idea at every dinner since you've known them? Or dreaming about the same trip to see the northern lights in Iceland for a decade but isn't a single step closer to pulling the trigger?

Permission pending is the default setting for a single person. As long as we can convince ourselves we're waiting for another person to shoulder the burden and give us permission, we can stay stagnant today, assuming our singleness is the problem.

Well, when I get married, I'll . . .

As I sat in the coffee shop, scheming up a sermon to help single people start playing offense, I wanted that to be the starting point: Permission granted.

I thought about my friend Jenelle.

She has a desire to be married but an even greater desire to be a foster mother. A few years ago, she realized she didn't need to wait for permission or marriage to foster.

Today she's a foster mother. It's not always easy and often requires her to rely heavily on her community. But she's not just doing it; she's thriving in it—providing a safe home and loving family for kids when they need it most. She's changing lives and having her life changed in the process. One day, when she gets married, her husband will step into a dream she's already in the middle of living out. Why? Because she didn't wait for permission—permission granted.

You're the one who gets to decide where you want to live, what you want to do, what your vacations should look like. Of course, you'll have to figure out a whole bunch of obstacles (saving money, finding work, etc.), but giving yourself the green light is the first step.

How are you going to spend your time?
How are you going to spend your money?
How are you going to use your God-given talents?

You get to decide.

Maybe one of the biggest problems with singleness is we still approach it like a bunch of second graders, feeling like we need to raise our hands and ask permission to live our lives.

Well, once I have a spouse, we'll be able to give each other permission to follow our dreams.

Or . . . you can give yourself permission to start chasing your dreams today. Flip the script—permission granted.

As I sat in the coffee shop, scribbling notes for my sermon, a second thought hatched in my mind. A memory about a conversation I'd recently had on a flight.

Burden/Blessing

I was sitting next to an eager extrovert. One of those guys that made it known he was looking for a sparring partner before I even fastened my seatbelt.

"So, is Austin home, or are you heading there to visit?" Classic plane question.

The questions slowly headed from shallow water to the deep end. I found out he and his wife (who had her headphones on and was staring out the window, happy to pass the ball to me for a few hours) were flying to Austin to meet their grandkid for the first time.

I congratulated them and asked him a few questions about his marriage, his kids, and his grandson, and the man's eyes lit up. He told me all about him, showed me pictures, and described the gift he'd gotten for the baby in extreme detail.

Then, like any decent human, he threw the ball back to me: "Are you married?"

A simple question.
A polite question.
That I wish he hadn't asked.

I panicked. My mind shut down, calling all the guards who have sworn to protect my own silly kingdom to attention.

In his book *7 Myths About Singleness*, Sam Allberry put good language to what we feel in that moment: "Marriage is a conversational intersection, with all sorts of interesting avenues of discussion. Singleness is more of a conversational cul-de-sac, requiring an awkward maneuver to exit."[3] I didn't want to shut the conversation down, but my lifestyle was about to throw us into a cul-de-sac.

Sam's quote reminds me of a night I got caught in a cul-de-sac. When I was a teenager, my friends and I used to chuck toilet paper all over random houses and call it fun. It's funny the things we find exciting when we're young. During one night of shenanigans, my friends were in the car standing guard while I was out doing all the dirty work. My heart stopped when I heard the car doors slam and my friends peel out, leaving me stranded. The next thing I knew, I was blinded by another set of headlights— a neighbor getting home to a newly altered lawn as I walked by with ten rolls stuffed in different pockets.

"Decorating for free?" he asked out his car window, a cold tone to his voice.

"Ah . . . no. I'm not sure what you are talking about," I said, continuing to walk away. I'm not good at lying as an adult; I was even worse as a kid. I just kept walking farther down the sidewalk with my head down. He kept pace with me, creeping alongside me until he finally stopped. I picked up speed, counting the cracks in the sidewalk, hoping to put as many as I could between us. To my relief, I heard him throw the car in park. He wasn't following. I kept counting—*thirty-five, thirty-six*—until I thought I was in the clear.

"Still here." The icy tone sent a chill down my spine. I wasn't getting away. It turned out, I was walking in a long, drawn-out circle around a cul-de-sac.

"I'm sorry," I finally said. "My friends and I are just being idiots." That made him laugh at least long enough for me to walk past his car. Then I took off at a dead sprint before he changed his mind, scanning yards for the best fence to jump in case it came to that.

When you're single, small talk inevitably feels like it's leading to a cul-de-sac. A dead end. A trap. "Oh no, I'm actually single," you say, then watch people panic and start telling you how sorry they are, as if you just told them someone in your family died. You don't want them to respond that way, they don't want to respond that way, but the conversation is stuck in a cul-de-sac. Either they tell you about a friend that was single for a long time but then found someone, or they try to set you up with their spouse's old college roommate.

Meanwhile, you sit there feeling like a burden. *Hey, thanks for trying. I'm just going to put in my headphones now.*

Here's the good news: It's all in the response. You aren't doomed to be a burden in every social setting; you can flip the script. Turn that cul-de-sac into a superhighway with all sorts of new and interesting exits.

So this is my new answer: "I've actually been a single pastor for a decade, which is a super unique space."

Suddenly a conversation ender becomes a conversation starter.
It's like putting the ball on the tee and handing them the driver.
Drop your equivalent to that line, and they have a whole bunch of
new questions they can ask.

I used to dread being asked if I was married, but now I love it.
Similarities are overrated. Differences make people interesting.
Turn the burden into a blessing.

Here's another example: being a third wheel.

I've driven a three-wheeler only once. I was twelve, and my family
and I were visiting some friends who had fifty acres in Michigan.
When we showed up, they had a brand-new toy waiting for us.
A three-wheeler that went just as fast as a quad but was way less
stable.

"Just don't turn too fast," they said, giving me the world's shortest
tutorial as I strapped on a helmet. "As long as you remember that,
you're good."

Got it.

The power gripped me as soon as I took off and quickly went to
my head. I zoomed around the property—faster and faster—
pushing the limits. Too caught up in the ecstasy to see the steep
hill I was about to drop in on until it was too late. I knew I
couldn't go straight down it, so I tried to turn left, but remembering the one instruction in my tutorial, I didn't want to turn too
fast. I ran out of real estate and hit the hill sideways. The machine
immediately flipped, throwing me to the ground and then top-
pling over me.

It was the first moment I ever felt everything go into slow motion,
and I managed to catch the machine as it rolled over me, keep
most of the weight off my body, and throw it past me as it contin-

ued to topple down the hill. The crew watched it all and sprinted my way, but by the time they got there, we were all laughing about my mistake.

Here's the point: The third wheel is tough.

If I'd been riding a dirt bike, I would've swerved and avoided the hill altogether. If I'd been on a quad, I would've headed right down the hill and been fine.

Two wheels are fast.
Four wheels are stable.
Three wheels are a challenge.

And as I've always said, what's true about motorized vehicles is true about life.

One couple going out to dinner is date night.
Two couples going out to dinner is a group date.
Me tagging along with a couple going out to dinner is uncomfortable.

Most of my friends are married, so I find myself in that situation often. The longer you're single, the more opportunities you'll have to turn an even number into an odd number.

"Thanks for dining with us this evening. Are you waiting on one more?"

No.

The empty chair sits next to you all night, reminding you you're alone. In uncomfortable situations, you naturally resort to thinking about yourself. Talking about your latest revelation while the couple you're with glances at each other, wondering what they're doing at this dinner as the three-wheeler tumbles down the hill.

Back in the coffee shop, I sat writing my sermon, giggling and reminiscing about all the times I'd been an awkward third wheel. Then I started thinking about how to help people flip the script. Turn the burden of the third wheel into a blessing.

Jesus mastered the craft. What was his secret? He turned conversations to be about the person he was talking to. Think about that moment in Luke 10 when a lawyer stood up to test him with a question about Scripture. Most of us would get defensive and try to show him that we know our stuff, but Jesus turned the question back on him and responded, "How do you read it?"[4]

If you can learn to ask really good questions, the attention won't be on the empty chair next to you. Instead, all the attention will be on the two full chairs across from you.

Start with some level one questions: "What's new in your life?" And then shift to level two: "What do you love about each other?" And then, if you're feeling crazy, put that three-wheeler into third gear: "What's one thing you're learning about yourself by being with each other?"

When you're flying solo, you have a unique opportunity to turn things back on the couple and get them to take a deep dive into their relationship. The empty fourth chair doesn't have to be a relational burden; it can be a blessing. You just have to flip the script.

By the time that clicked for me in the coffee shop, I'd already emptied my second cup of coffee. The dam was broken. I couldn't type fast enough to keep up with all the ideas popping into my mind—decades of frustrations and thoughts spilling out of a deep well in my soul.

Quick/Acquired

A while back, some good friends of mine gifted me seven days at an all-inclusive resort in Mexico to work on this book.

Staying at an all-inclusive by yourself is an amazing experience, but only if you're prepared for it. You have to be ready to laugh easily, because the week will give you plenty of opportunities to resort back to grasping. Between the honeymooners and the couples-themed shows at night, every day basically feels like Valentine's Day.

If you can get past caring about that, it's phenomenal.

If you're going to give it a shot, there's one phrase you have to get really used to saying. Repeat after me: "Table for one, please." Try it out. How'd it feel? Now say it again. This time, picture the host thinking you're joking. And then slowly her smile turns into confusion, which eventually becomes sadness. Jonah Hill's character in *Forgetting Sarah Marshall* masterfully portrays this moment when he says, "Do you want, like, a magazine or something? It's gonna be boring if you're just sitting by yourself."[5]

One evening I went to dinner at a Japanese restaurant where the chef prepared everything at the table. Pro tip: If the table-for-one thing makes you uncomfortable, avoid those restaurants like the plague. Because your table for one will actually be a table for ten surrounding a large stove. Odds are, you'll have a family of four on your left and a family of four on your right. Both families will be staring at you the whole dinner because you'll be in the middle, with an empty seat next to you. And they won't know what to say. Either they'll assume your date is sick in the hotel room and stare at you like you're a monster. Or they'll assume you got your heart broken earlier that day and stare at you with pity.

As for me, I had one of those families on my left and another on my right.

The food, however, was delicious. Our chef was named Luis, and he came out guns blazing, throwing knives up in the air while the whole stove went up in flames and tossing broccoli to us to catch in our mouths like we were birds at a zoo. Each bite was better than the last—tender, fresh, and, best of all, free. All of us watched in awe as Luis prepared a five-star dinner for us to enjoy.

All of us, except the eight-year-old kid next to me. He ordered a hot dog and fries.

Honestly, I respected it. A power move if I'd ever seen one. Save your onion volcano and knife tricks, Luis. Just roll up some pork and stick it in a microwave for forty-five seconds. Medium-rare filet? How about some three-day-old saltless fries?

Over the next hour, we enjoyed a five-course meal while the kid ate a plain hot dog—no ketchup, no mustard, thank you very much. And then he fell asleep in his chair before dessert, which made me laugh really hard all the way back to my room.

Singleness, much like fine dining, is an acquired taste. There's the quick fix, and then there's the real, deep contentment you can learn to love.

We aren't built for singleness. Have I mentioned it's not good for us to be alone? At first, you aren't going to like it. Keep your eyes open at an all-inclusive resort, and you'll spot a moody teenager with their AirPods in who can't enjoy their family vacation because it's pulling them away from their crush for a few days. All the dolphins and sunsets in the world won't be enough to get them out of their lovesick rut. They have an opportunity to enjoy a five-course meal by the sea, but instead, they're settling for a lukewarm hot dog.

We may all be that moody teenager at some point, trying to figure out all the hormones, but we don't have to stay there. We can learn to love the deep connections we can find with our Creator, with creation, with friends, and with ourselves.

We can love life without a love life!

Eating healthy isn't easy at first, but if you keep going, one day at a time, your body will start to love the nutrition and your taste buds will adjust and begin craving salads over sugar.

In the same way, solitude starts out challenging. Sit in silence for ten minutes, and you'll feel like you're losing your mind. But do it again tomorrow and the next day, and it'll start getting easier. Before you know it, you'll start looking forward to it.

Or think about purity. Purity is an acquired taste. Many of us grew up hearing that it was a requirement. Maybe you're over it now that you're an adult, and to avoid the shame that comes with chasing it, you dismiss it as legalistic or oppressive. The truth is, there's a third way. There's a lifestyle on the other side of all that baggage. A pursuit of purity without all the religious shame is possible. It's an acquired taste, but it feels a lot like freedom.

Acquire the taste for singleness, and you just may meet someone who has done the same.

Or you may not. Either way, you'll be content.

Control/Surrender

"We are moving almost 67,000 miles an hour." Professor S took his glasses off and shook the cramp out of his hand. "Do you understand that?"

We all nodded and said we did, but we didn't. At least not at the same level as he did, frantically scribbling numbers and diagrams on the chalkboard. "Right now, as you sit in this lecture hall staring at me, we are flying through space. Our planet is a spacecraft, and it travels over a million miles every day."

Astronomy was one of my favorite classes in college. Mostly because of Professor S's passion. (I can't remember his real name, but if you have to come up with a name for your astronomy teacher, *Professor S* feels right, doesn't it?) The guy's love for space was contagious.

"When you read your textbook tonight, remember, at the end of each sentence we will have traveled another hundred miles in the time it took you to read it."

Of course, the only thing he was wrong about was his belief that any of us actually did the reading.

"It gets stranger," he warned. His bushy eyebrows matched the thickness of his beard, and all the hair on his face stood up straight. "As the earth moves around the sun, our solar system is soaring through space at 448,000 miles per hour—Los Angeles to London in under a minute. Meanwhile, most of you are thinking about how bored you are in this lecture hall."

I thoroughly enjoyed that lecture. Because (whether or not Professor S agrees) I'm pretty convinced that all of that happened not by default but by design. It's not an accident. It's a masterpiece—the work of an Artist with a tremendous amount of creativity.

And that Artist, the one who spoke all of this into existence with a few words, the one who measures the heavens with the span of his hand[6] and puts the oceans in jars,[7] also knows the number of hairs on your head[8] and cares about the small things in your life.[9]

Think about that for a second.
That's crazy.
Really crazy.

Meanwhile, I'm down here on earth freaking out about my reputation, my ten-year plan, and whether or not I'm ruining God's
plans because I'm not all that interested in dating.

By this point, the coffee shop had been closed for twenty minutes.
I was outside, looking up into the night sky, thankful for a sermon I was writing a hundred times faster than normal, and
thinking back on Professor S's epic lecture.

When I boil this whole singleness journey down to the core, I realize how much I want to be in control. I want to be in charge of
my life. With a little perspective, that control begins to look pretty
silly. As if the night sky is always winking at us, showing us the
way out of our own skull-sized kingdom.

I've noticed that in the moments when I feel lonely, upset, or anxious, I'm not thinking about just how absurd this whole thing is.
I'm an incredibly small and insignificant part of this story, yet I'm
infinitely more valuable than you could ever imagine. And freedom for single people exists somewhere in that tension.

Because the same thing is true about you. You're just a small piece
of this giant puzzle, yet you're eternally significant. God sees you,
loves you, and cares about your singleness even when it may not
feel like it. Maybe you've been praying for a spouse for years, but
you're still single. God's timeline doesn't always make sense, and
there aren't easy answers to why it doesn't. I believe the wait will
be worth it in hindsight, but in the middle of it, it sure doesn't feel
that way, does it?

That's why this whole topic is so tricky and why it took an entire
book to get to this point. Let's just be real: Romantic love is one of

the most beautiful, mysterious, compelling parts of life. There's a
reason romance plays a part in every story ever told. There's a
reason love is a topic of conversation every time friends catch up.
It's because love helps us make sense of a confusing world. Unfortunately, that also means when you're single, this confusing world
can feel downright chaotic.

You know God has a plan, but you begin to wonder if he left you
out of it.
You know things can change, but you begin to doubt they ever
will.
And you know people mean well, but you begin to worry that if
one more married person tells you to just be patient and trust
God's timing, you're going to lose your mind.

There are a lot of good answers to singleness, but there are very
few great ones. Most feel like cold comfort—a small sip of water
in a desert. It seems one of the only true answers to singleness is
to follow Jesus's radical invitation to stop worrying about tomorrow and be present today. To let go of the past and the future and
trust that the One who hung the constellations in the night sky is
present with you right here, right now.[10] To stop trying to figure it
all out and start trusting the bigger story going on. All you have
to do is look up at those balls of gas burning billions of miles
away and then glance over at the moon hanging out 238,900
miles above us, keeping the tides in our oceans rising and falling,
and all the defense you play trying to protect your own little kingdom will feel silly—a feeble attempt at control.

Meanwhile, the One who made it all invites you to the sweet
freedom of surrender.

To the laughing on the other side of the grasping.
To the wonder on the other side of the selfishness.
To the healing on the other side of naming and feeling pain from
the past.

To the deep exhale the night sky gifts you as it pulls you up out of your kingdom and gives you some perspective.

The world is a scary place, especially when you're a solo traveler. It's natural to try to find some comfort in control, but you can flip the script on your singleness. You can confront yesterday, surrender tomorrow, and embrace today. It's not easy, but when you start acquiring a taste for surrender, contentment in the present moment becomes possible.

When you do the hard work to stir the water in your soul . . .
And still it . . .
And share it . . .
One today at a time . . .
Singleness becomes really fun.

If you keep going—on repeat—you'll wake up one morning, look in the mirror, and realize you're genuinely thankful for this gift of singleness you've been given. You won't spend the whole day replaying yesterday, worrying about tomorrow, or obsessing over whether something is wrong with you.

In fact, you probably won't be thinking about yourself much at all.

You'll be too busy enjoying being single today.

Mary's Interlude (Act 3)

Share What You Have

Dinner didn't feel like enough. She knew Jesus didn't need any thanks, but it still felt like an insignificant gift for the One who had given them their brother back.

Lazarus sat to the Rabbi's left, smiling. He hadn't stopped smiling since the incident. Since he had gone to his grave for four days, leaving them alone to weep and mourn until Jesus showed up and he began breathing again. He still wouldn't tell her much about the experience. He was a man of few words these days, who just laughed a lot and always seemed to be enjoying the present moment.

Conversation flowed freely. The crew spoke to Mary like she was an old friend, and to her excitement, Mary realized she did the same.

These moments used to feel forced. Keeping conversations going, exchanging pleasantries, and making people feel welcome—it all used to feel awkward and clumsy. The voices in her head would judge her for everything she said, like the Sanhedrin examining her words in order to condemn her as a social outcast.

You're too quiet.
You're too loud.
That was out of place.
That wasn't funny.
You're boring.

They don't care.
There must be something wrong with you.

The voices were gone now.

A new lease on her brother's life was only one of the gifts Jesus had given them. He'd given all of them their lives back, each in their own way. Mary thought back to the days before that fateful dinner, the call to more. They felt like another life, and in some strange way, they were. She'd learned so much about what actually mattered (and what didn't) in the past few years. She'd experienced the freedom found in getting her eyes off her own little kingdom.

Abundant life, she thought to herself. *The greatest gift one can receive.*

She knew dinner was more than enough for the Rabbi, yet it didn't feel anywhere near adequate. *What gift could ever be enough?*

Mary's legs started moving before her mind fully figured out why. Pure joy pulsed through her veins as she dropped her plate and took off like lightning. She raced into her room, grabbed a jar of perfume, and rejoined the group in the main dining area.

Her sister and brother saw the jar in her hands and eyed her suspiciously. They knew this was her most prized possession, her life's savings, easily worth three hundred days of work, but she didn't care. Money didn't matter. She'd learned a new way to live. A life of surrender, of sacrifice, and of using the gifts she'd been given to bless others.

Mary broke open the jar, and the sweet smell of the oil filled every crevice of the home. She'd longed to experience that smell for years, but now she barely noticed it. Too excited to stop and enjoy it, she used every last drop to anoint Jesus's feet as everyone stared in disbelief. Jesus simply smiled. He nodded as if he understood Mary's motivations better than she did.

An unbridled, unbounded joy began to well up in the depths of Mary's soul. A deeper joy than she'd ever felt exploded up from within and turned to laughter.

Mistakes from yesterday, worry about tomorrow—none of it mattered. She'd spend the rest of her days generously sharing her gift with the world. Freely she had been given; freely she'd give.

The last drop had spilled out of the jar by the time Mary finally looked up. Every eye was on her. Some, including Jesus, joined in the laughter.

One man, however, stood in the back of the room, shaking his head. Mary knew the man, although she had said very few words to him. Judas spoke up, condemning her for the foolishness.

Mary barely heard a word.

She wasn't listening.
She didn't care.
She now knew you couldn't put a price on connection.

Mary and You

By Mary's third interaction with Jesus, I love how sold out she appears to have been. According to Judas, that perfume was worth an entire year's wages.[1] Yet Mary didn't even hesitate to share it all with Jesus.

Whether or not Mary was really single, what we know for certain is that she was fully committed to the cause. She'd realized by this point that life wasn't about building her own little kingdom; it was about being a part of the kingdom of heaven. And she played her part well by sharing what she had.

My hope in part 3 has been to inspire you to be like Mary. Your life is a tremendous gift, and gifts are for sharing. The question isn't, *How long am I going to be single?* The question is, *How can I share this gift with the world?*

For Reflection and Discussion

1. What is one way you can be like Mary and share your gift of singleness with the world today?

2. Do you believe your singleness is a gift? What is one aspect of your singleness that you haven't been taking full advantage of? How can you lean into that advantage today?

3. Did part 3 change your perspective on conflict in any way? How do you handle conflict? Is there a way you're avoiding conflict? If so, how is that affecting your relationships?

4. Do you ever feel lonely in your singleness? When does that loneliness tend to set in? What is one new place you can go to find some community this week?

5. Is there something you've been waiting for permission for? How can you practice being fully present today by giving yourself permission to take a step forward?

Epilogue

Single-Minded

A few weeks after that day I sat in a coffee shop and decided to finally start talking about my experiences being single, I spent an entire Sunday preaching a message called "Flip the Script on Singleness." It was 9:30 P.M. by the time our third service ended and everyone left. I set the alarm, locked the door, and sat in another empty church parking lot.

Same Chevy Cruze.
Same night of the week.
Same deep exhaustion after a long day of church.

But this time, I was actually able to cry. And the tears weren't from sadness or frustration; they were happy tears. Tears of gratitude, like rivers of living water welling from the depths of my soul and running down my face—water I was sharing with the world.

Singleness wasn't something I felt shame about anymore; it was something I was proud of. Passionate about. I'd just spent the day standing on a stage for three services, talking about it earnestly instead of reluctantly. Speaking from a place of deep conviction that singleness doesn't have to be a burden; it can be a blessing.

I glanced around the empty parking lot and then up into the night sky. The stars looked brighter. The music sounded fuller, more emotive. I could feel again. Love, joy, excitement, and a deep, powerful peace that transcended circumstances—a reminder that I'm okay.

There isn't something wrong with me.

The tears were an overflow of the gratitude I felt for the journey that had brought me there.

After a few minutes, I whispered a prayer, thanking God for everything, then effortlessly put my car in drive and headed home.

The more I talked about singleness, the more stories I began to hear. Stories from amazing single people. Some who are single for a reason, others who are single for a season. Some who want to be single for the rest of their lives, others who are praying their singleness comes to an end tomorrow. Some who have been single for decades, others who are single for the first time in decades.

Person after person.

Each with their own story but a common thread summed up in one word: *potential.*

Singleness is a gift under the tree. Inside the box is a whole bunch of potential. Potential you can choose to tap into or ignore. This book is my best attempt at convincing you to choose the former.

The world needs your gifts, your personality, and your stories. It's not the same without you. And you don't have to wait for a partner to begin sharing. Don't be double-minded; be single-minded by doubling down on where you are today!

Press into it.
Celebrate it.
Appreciate it.

Because whatever comes in the future, I'm convinced we'll never regret making the most of where we are right now.

Stir the water.
Still the water.
Share the water.

Every chance you get, remind the world that wants to keep you stuck in your past or worried about your future that you're too busy being single today. And the next time someone asks if you have the gift of singleness, but you know they're really asking if you think you're going to be single the rest of your life, smile and politely explain to them that your singleness is a gift and so is today.

Acknowledgments

Writing is a team sport, and I'm spoiled. I have the world's best teammates.

Doug Wekenman: For being there every step of the way. I had to stop myself from including a Doug story in every chapter, but I could've.

Mom and Dad: For reading the first draft of this book and pushing me to take a risk and release it.

Ethan Matott: For your incredible ability to infuse humor into all the situations I overthink. I can't wait to read your afterword for this one.

Matt Fons: For always asking excellent questions. And, of course, for that conversation in Hawaii.

Bryan Bartolome, Jenelle Cherek, and Samarah Larrain: For letting me read the opening chapters out loud to you. You were the first to hear them. Until that night, I thought this book was only for me. You all are the reason the rest of the world is reading it too.

Kory Miller: For that dinner in Laguna Beach and the decision to go pro.

Justin Matott: For teaching me how to set aside my insecurities and write.

Shawn Johnson: For never even hesitating for a second to champion me as a single pastor.

Kyle Negrete: For all those dinners at Polvos. And for being a great agent and friend.

Sam Wekenman: For proofreading everything I write. I promise I'll figure out commas one of these days.

Gary Bruegman: For believing in me, pushing me to write, and being a picture of both grace and truth in my life.

Keith Garton: For all the stories we get to tell together.

Jeff Tacklind: For teaching me how to write from the deep places.

Jacob Phillips and Johnny Shinnick: For all your vision, inspiration, and hard work with this book's creative elements.

Sam and Rebecca Ellis: For all the prayers, support, and encouragement. Our dinners in Fallbrook are some of my favorite evenings.

Kevin and Elisa Bill: For gifting me that writing week in Mexico and for being a picture of generosity.

Nick Rush and Wes Eggett: For coming up with that angsty line "Love life without the love life" during the Static Rebellion garage band years. It was like a seed planted fourteen years before I started writing this book.

Susan Tjaden: For believing in this book from day one and for all your brilliant thoughts along the way.

Will Anderson, Luverta Reames, Jamie Lapeyrolerie, Elizabeth Groening, and Leslie Calhoun: For reading an early draft and offering so much helpful insight.

Campbell Wharton: For that impromptu meeting in New York. I still can't believe we ran into each other at that coffee shop.

Tina Constable: For taking the time to listen to my story and believe in this message.

The entire WaterBrook team: For working so hard to make this book matter.

Notes

Introduction: Two Enemies of Singleness
1. Thirty-two percent of stats are made up.

Part 1: Yesterday
1. Genesis 2:18.

Chapter 1: Stagnant Water
1. Genesis 1:28.
2. John 5:1–4.
3. John 5:7.
4. Or thrice.
5. Bag End is the name of the home that Bilbo Baggins (and later Frodo Baggins) lived in.
6. John 7:37–38.

Chapter 2: The Ones That Got Away
1. Lonestar, "Amazed," track 3 on *Lonely Grill*, BNA Records, 1999.
2. Garth Brooks has a famous song called "Unanswered Prayers" about the moment he realized he was thankful that an old relationship hadn't worked out.
3. John 4:1–29.
4. Craig Groeschel (@CraigGroeschel), Twitter, May 9, 2022, https://twitter.com/craiggroeschel/status/1523603702732529665?lang=en.
5. Genesis 2:18.
6. To be clear, this is just a joke. I know I stepped into decades of debate about what Gandalf meant by "fly." For the record, I tend to think he was telling them to get over their shock and run.

7. John 4:18.
8. John 8:32.

Chapter 3: Sex, Shame, and Stoners

1. "How Porn Can Affect the Brain like a Drug," Fight the New Drug, accessed June 27, 2023, https://fightthenewdrug.org/how-porn-can -affect-the-brain-like-a-drug.
2. Genesis 1:28.
3. Ingrid Solano, Nicholas R. Eaton, and K. Daniel O'Leary, "Pornography Consumption, Modality, and Function in a Large Internet Sample," *Journal of Sex Research* 57, no. 1 (2020): 92–103, https:// doi.org/10.1080/00224499.2018.1532488.
4. Genesis 2:24.
5. Matthew 28:19.
6. Matthew 5:27–28.
7. Matthew 5:29.
8. Matthew 19:4–6.
9. John 7:37–38.
10. John 8:2–11.
11. Julie Andrews, vocalist, "A Spoonful of Sugar," in *Mary Poppins,* directed by Robert Stevenson (Burbank, Calif.: Walt Disney Productions, 1964).
12. John 8:10–11.
13. Mark Chamberlain, quoted in Jacob Hess, "Why You Keep Going Back to Porn After Trying to Quit," Fight the New Drug, accessed June 28, 2023, https://fightthenewdrug.org/why-you-keep-going -back-to-porn-after-trying-to-quit.
14. Romans 7:19.
15. 1 John 3:1.
16. "Why Porn Can Be Difficult to Quit," Fight the New Drug, accessed June 28, 2023, https://fightthenewdrug.org/why-porn-can-be -difficult-to-quit.
17. Luke 1:78–79, NLT.

Chapter 4: The Happiest Place on Earth

1. "The Grand Opening of Disneyland," Designing Disney, accessed June 28, 2023, www.designingdisney.com/parks/disneyland-resort /grand-opening-disneyland.
2. Neal Gabler, *Walt Disney: The Triumph of the American Imagination* (New York: Vintage Books, 2007), 605.
3. Gabler, *Walt Disney*, 606.
4. "Land Cover Change," NOAA Office for Coastal Management, accessed July 7, 2023, https://coast.noaa.gov/states/fast-facts/land -cover-change.html.
5. "Vector-Borne Diseases," World Health Organization, March 2, 2020, www.who.int/news-room/fact-sheets/detail/vector-borne -diseases; "Fighting the World's Deadliest Animal," Centers for Disease Control and Prevention, August 15, 2019, www.cdc.go /globalhealth/stories/2019/world-deadliest-animal.html.
6. Christopher Lucas, quoted in "Disney's Magic Kingdom Was Mapped Out by a General You've Never Heard Of," *Tampa Bay Times*, February 15, 2021, www.tampabay.com/news/business /2021/02/15/disneys-magic-kingdom-was-mapped-out-by-a -general-youve-never-heard-of.
7. Christopher Lucas, *Top Disney: 100 Top Ten Lists of the Best of Disney, from the Man to the Mouse and Beyond* (Guilford, Conn.: Lyons, 2019), 32.
8. "Why Are There No Mosquitoes at Disney World?," *Top Villas* (blog), Top Villas, www.thetopvillas.com/blog/disney-world/why -are-there-no-mosquitoes-at-disney-world.
9. Genesis 15:5, CSB.
10. James 3:16, NLT.
11. James Clear, *Atomic Habits: An Easy & Proven Way to Build Good Habits & Break Bad Ones* (New York: Avery, 2018), 27.

Chapter 5: The Tomorrow Trap

1. 1 Corinthians 7:7.
2. Matthew 6:34, NLT.

Chapter 6: Bring the Wine

1. John 2:1–11.
2. John 2:7.
3. John Eldredge, *Beautiful Outlaw: Experiencing the Playful, Disruptive, Extravagant Personality of Jesus* (New York: FaithWords, 2011), 58.
4. This is a reference to season 3, episode 16 of *The Office*. It's a classic episode, where Michael Scott tries to make Phyllis and Bob's wedding about him.
5. Luke 15:1–32.
6. John McClintock and James Strong, eds., *Cyclopaedia of Biblical, Theological, and Ecclesiastical Literature* (New York: Harper & Brothers, 1894), 8:68.
7. Luke 15:31.
8. Mark 2:19.

Chapter 7: Less Grasping, More Laughing

1. Matthew 6:34, NLT.
2. Matthew 6:33–34.

Mary's Interlude (Act 2)

1. John 11:35.
2. Hebrews 13:5.

Chapter 9: The Kingdom of Me

1. Matthew 4:17.
2. Genesis 2:18.
3. C. S. Lewis, *Mere Christianity* (New York: HarperOne, 2001), 227.
4. Acts 4:13.

Chapter 11: Single, Not Alone

1. John Mulaney, "John Mulaney Monologue—SNL," *Saturday Night Live*, YouTube video, 8:21, www.youtube.com/watch?v=jRLH8E_CpP0&t=169s.
2. Timothy Keller, *The Meaning of Marriage: Facing the Complexities of Commitment with the Wisdom of God* (New York: Riverhead Books, 2013), 101.

3.   John 21:25.
4.   Revelation 7:9.

Chapter 12: Flip the Script on Singleness

1.   *Remember the Titans,* directed by Boaz Yakin (Burbank, Calif.: Walt Disney Pictures, 2000).
2.   Matthew 16:18, ESV.
3.   Sam Allberry, *7 Myths About Singleness* (Wheaton, Ill.: Crossway, 2019), 12.
4.   Luke 10:26.
5.   *Forgetting Sarah Marshall,* directed by Nicholas Stoller (Universal City, Calif.: Universal Pictures, 2008).
6.   Isaiah 40:12.
7.   Psalm 33:7.
8.   Luke 12:7.
9.   1 Peter 5:7.
10. Job 9:9.

Mary's Interlude (Act 3)

1.   John 12:5.

Ryan Wekenman is a thirtysomething storyteller and single pastor who passionately believes we don't have to be married to live wholly. Ryan has a master's degree from Talbot School of Theology. He co-hosts a popular podcast, *Stories in Scripture*, that brings the Bible to life for people all around the world. Ryan lives in Austin, Texas, where he helped plant Red Rocks Austin, a young, vibrant church full of people who are ready to change the world.

You can find out more about his work at ryanwekenman.com.

About the Type

This book was set in Minion, a 1990 Adobe Originals typeface by Robert Slimbach. Minion is inspired by classical, old-style typefaces of the late Renaissance, a period of elegant and beautiful type designs. Created primarily for text setting, Minion combines the aesthetic and functional qualities that make text type highly readable with the versatility of digital technology.